CLASSIC AUTHOR BIOGRAPHY SERIES

LEW WALLACE AND THE STORY OF *BEN-HUR*

Joseph Leininger Wheeler, PhD

FaithHappenings Publishers

Copyright © 2016 Joseph Leininger Wheeler

This book was first published as part of the work *Ben-Hur,* Focus on the Family Great Stories Series (Wheaton, IL: Tyndale House Publishers, 1997).

All rights reserved. No part of this publication may be reproduced, distributed or transmitted in any form or by any means, including photocopying, recording, or other electronic or mechanical methods, without the prior written permission of the publisher, except in the case of brief quotations embodied in critical reviews and certain other noncommercial uses permitted by copyright law.

FaithHappenings Publishers
7061 S. University Blvd., Suite 307
Centennial, CO 80122

Cover Design ©2016 FaithHappenings Publishers.
Illustration credits: "Lew Wallace." Herringshaw, Thomas W. *Prominent Men and Women of the Day* (Chicago: Home Publishing House, 1888). Original text owned by Joe Wheeler.
Book Layout ©2013 BookDesignTemplates.com

Illustrations in the book come from the following sources: Wallace, Lew. *The Chariot Race from Ben-Hur.* (New York: Harper & Brothers, 1908). Original text owned by Joe Wheeler.
Wallace, Lew. *Ben-Hur: The Player's Edition* (New York: Harper & Brothers, 1908). Original text owned by Joe Wheeler.

Lew Wallace and the Story of *Ben-Hur* -- 1st ed.
ISBN 978-1-941555-14-9
This book was printed in the United States of America.

To order additional copies of this book, contact:
info@faithhappenings.com

FaithHappenings Publishers,
a division of FaithHappenings.com

BEN-HUR

INTRODUCTION

The Fascination of *Ben-Hur*

I was just a child when I first read *Ben-Hur*. But, like most children, I liked the book without really knowing why. After all, to a child, a book, a radio drama, a TV show, a movie—*all* is reality. When something is reality, rarely does one dissect it or ask *why* it's real. Criticism comes with age.

When a teenager, I read it again—and this time, it was the chariot racing I remember most vividly.

I read it again as a teacher, mainly because a student I had assigned it to complained of how slow it moved. Slow? *Ben-Hur*. Surely, he was kidding! But, to my surprise, at the beginning, the action was indeed a little slow. In fact, it remained so for about a quarter of the book; then, suddenly it was in gear—from that point on, it was virtually un-put-down-able. I determined that "some day," I'd find out why it was constructed that way. With the editing of this book, the second in this Series, arrived my moment of truth.

What I discovered was this: the reasons for its initial slowness are several; (1) there are actually two books grafted together—deliberately; (2) before the action could proceed non-stop, there had to be a lot of explaining first; (3) by the very nature of the time-frame (Christ's 33 years on earth), the characters would age much more during the story than is typical in such a book—that necessitated a character who would represent the glue which holds the narrative together; (4) most significant of all: the difficulties involved in introducing our Lord into a work of fiction. In mid to late Nineteenth Century, this just wasn't done! In fact, to many many Christians, *all* fiction was considered suspect, if not evil.

In getting ready for this edition, I read the book again—four times, in conjunction with the Garfield Edition and its 850 beautiful woodcut illustrations. This two-volume extravaganza cost $30 in 1891 (equivalent of paying $500 - $650 today), making it one of the most expensive such sets of its time—and today, incredibly rare.

This time, the combination of illustrations and multiple readings almost overwhelmed me: one of the most profound spiritual experiences of my life. Along the way, I discovered how very important it is that the reader digest *all* of it, for everything in the book builds on what has gone before—especially the love of the ancient world in the first section of the book. How Wallace put it all together represents one of the great miracles of American literature.

Next the movie. Well, Charlton Heston—he *IS* the 1959 movie. Larger than life. Like John Wayne, Heston has never been one for supporting actor roles: he dominates, takes over, is "realer" than most of the people we know in real life.

Which brings us to the problem of movie reality. Especially in terms of movies which purport to re-create actual history. It is a problem which Aldous Huxley first introduced via his World Controller in *Brave New World*: a dictator may—by the rather simple act of destroying all pertinent records of the past—actually *change* history: once historical records are destroyed, who can possibly mount a successful challenge to rewritten or distorted history? Movie producers don't even have to do this deliberately, for they can hide under the Protean blanket of "artistic license." Result: a movie which bears so little resemblance to the book it is supposedly based on that the author watches it in horror and disbelief! "Where did this monstrosity come from? Certainly not from *my* book!"

So it is that I find precious few movies based on works of literature . . . fail to disappoint. Well, to a certain extent, *all* movies disappoint for each of us, while reading, creates our own inner cinematography. No two of us transubstantiate abstract words into the same visual imagery—consequently, when we subsequently watch a movie based on the book, invariably somebody else's perception of what occurs in the story jars against our own. *Even*—which is rare indeed!—when the movie plot line mirrors the original perfectly. This is the reason why mystery writer Sue Grafton adamantly refuses to let her books be filmed.

What I'm getting to is this: is there not a grave danger here? Let's say that 100,000 people read a book—but, over time, 10,000,000 people see the movie. What will people remember? Even those who both read the book and watched the movie. Of course! There is virtually no contest: the visual celluloid imagery is so powerful and so lasting that it thunders down the mountain like a spring thaw avalanche, burying truth (as it was originally depicted) under a smothering, obliterating, blanket of fabrication.

In other words, the perception I, you, us gained from the great cimematic tour de force of the film, sweeping the Academy Awards—is not the truth as Lew Wallace perceived it. Not by a very long shot!

To get that, we must read the book—*carefully!*

SPECIAL NOTE

The sources that made this Introduction possible are these: *"Ben-Hur" Wallace: The Life of General Lew Wallace*, by Irving McKee, University of California Press, Berkeley, 1947; and *Lew Wallace, An Autobiography*, Harper and Brothers, New York, 1906, Volumes 1 and 2.

ILLUSTRATIONS FOR THIS BOOK

Fortunately, I have been able to secure both a copy of the original 1900 Harpers "Players Edition" of *Ben-Hur* with their vintage illustrations, as well as the 1908 Harpers edition of *The Chariot Race from Ben-Hur*. Together, they make this edition one-of-a-kind!

IRIS

BEN-HUR STAGE AND MOVIE HISTORY

Wallace didn't have to worry about movie screen-writer and movie producer story distortion during his lifetime, but he *did* have to worry about what live stage troupes would do to it. That is why he resisted for so many years those who wished to dramatize the book. First was the actor Lawrence Barrett, who, in 1882, was at the height of his fame. Wallace turned him down for a number of reasons: in the first case, he considered the theme too sacred—he had seen way too many examples of serious works reduced to slapstick and buffoonery by troupes eager to please sensation-seeking crowds; in the second case, he didn't see how the epic cast could possibly be successfully re-created on a standard stage; and, in the third case, quite probably Wallace—always the frustrated wannabee dramatist—wanted to write his own stage script.

Wallace blinked at Ellen K. Bradford's 1887 *Selections from Ben-Hur Adapted for Reading with Tableaux*, but did not sanction it. In 1889, he stepped in, in self-defense, with his own *Ben-Hur in Tableaux and Pantomime* for Walter C. Clark and D. W. Cox, who then toured the country with it.

But, for ambitious ventures, he continued to say no. No to actor and playwright Alexander Salvini. No to the brothers Imre and Bolossy Kiralfy, masters of extravaganza. Even no to British and German dramatists. By 1889, he finally became hard-nosed and threatened those who went ahead anyway with legal action.

But one man persisted: Early in the Eighties, young Abraham Erlanger bought a copy of *Ben-Hur*, read it, and fell in love with it, telling his then-manager, Joseph Jefferson, that someday he would produce that book. Fifteen years later, he and Marc Klaw had risen to the top, and their Theatrical Syndicate was helping to transform ma and pa drama to big business sophistication. Through Harpers, a meeting was set up with Wallace. Wallace was impressed, but still dubious and not a little apprehensive. He was up front with a deal-maker-or-breaker-absolute: *Christ must not be impersonated on the stage.* Erlanger was willing to accept . . . but . . . . He sent his agent/director, Joseph Brooks to Wallace's home; negotiated, explained, then accompanied Wallace by train to New York, where he showed him models of the sets and his proposed use of a 25,000 candlepower shaft of light to represent the presence of Christ.

Wallace then consulted with Christian thought-leaders, and continued to temporize. Three months later, after extensive negotiation back and forth, a legal agreement was at last signed: (1) the play would use the exact *Ben-Hur* text phraseology whenever possible; (2) neither the face nor figure of Christ could be depicted; (3) and Wallace was to receive $4\frac{2}{3}$% royalties.

Always the visionary, Wallace predicted, "You now have a subject which, properly outfitted, will last your lives, longer in fact than Uncle Tom." (McKee, P. 176). He was not far off, when one adds in movie portrayals.

William Young, originally from Chicago, an attorney as well as script-writer, was asked by Erlanger to see what he could do. He had already written *Pendragon* (1881) and *Rajah* (1883), with a record 250 performances, and a number of other very successful hits. Young spent half a year on *Ben-Hur*. He made a real effort to retain as much of the original dialogue as possible, and divided the play into a musical prelude and thirteen scenes (with six acts): (1) the desert (with pantomime of the Wise Men); (2) the roof of the Hur palace in Jerusalem; (3) the galley; (4) the raft; (5) Simonides' house; (6) the Grove of Daphne; (7) the Fountain of Castalia; (8) Sheik Ilderim's tent; (9) the Orchard of Palms; (10) the gateway to the Circus; (11) the arena; (12) the Vale of Hinnom; and

(13) the Mount of Olives. The light—waxing, to signify the approach of Christ; waning to show His exit—appeared in the last scene (McKee. pp. 176-7).

Edgar Stillman Kelley (a New York College of Music professor) composed the choir-chants, a camel motif, a theme for Christ, ballet accompaniment, anthems of praise." (McKee, p. 177). To create realistic-looking waves, Claude L. Hagen was hired on; he also devised a sort of treadmill for the original chariot race, and a moving panorama.

The casting was a bit turbulent: Edward J. Morgan (he had elicited raves as John Storm in *The Christian)* replaced at the last minute, Walter Whiteside as Ben-Hur. Esther's role too was difficult to finalize: Gretchen Lyons replacing Grace George. Henry Irving never completely forgave his agent for discouraging him in *his* desire to play Simonides; Henry Lee stepped in. Messala's role initially went to a young man, subsequently to become a movie great, William S. Hart. But he was quickly elevated to the lead part, Ben-Hur. Iras was played by Corona Ricardo.

What kind of excitement was generated by all this? Well, let's let McKee chronicle it:

> "A great deal of interest was shown throughout the week," said the New York *Clipper*, late in 1899, "in the coming production of *Ben-Hur*. General Lew Wallace, the author of the novel, arrived in town to watch the final rehearsals of the play, and to be present at the first performance, on November 29. There was an eager demand for seats, and a long line of purchasers was daily in evidence after the opening of the sale, with the exception of the Irving engagement, the largest of the season." Advance publicity heralded the biggest play ever attempted; Erlanger had invested the unprecedented amount of $75,000; the treadmills alone coast $15,000, and the company numbered four hundred. At one of the dress rehearsals—there were two

weeks of them, after four weeks of the ordinary kind—Charles Frohman said to Klaw and Erlanger: "Boys, I'm afraid you're up against it—the American public will never stand for Christ and a horse race in the same show." Frohman was trying to buy an interest in the play.

The premiere at the vast Broadway Theater was a prodigy, even for New York (and with such distinguished competition as Richard Mansfield in *Cyrano de Bergerac*; John Drew in *The Tyranny of Tears*; Julia Marlowe in *Barbara Frietchie*; Anna Held in *Papa's Wife*; Mrs. Fiske in *Becky Sharp*; William Gillette in *Sherlock Holmes*). "Not before, in this season or last—perhaps not before in a decade," hazarded the *World*, "has New York had a theatrical production around which such keen and widespread interest has centered." All the standing room was stood upon. The places of many of the regular first-nighters were filled by "nice folks" whose faces were strange, quipped the *Times*. General Wallace himself, surrounded by a half-dozen ladies, was the center of attention as he sat in the front of a lower proscenium box....

First came the orchestral prelude. Then, in quick succession: The tableau of the Wise Men and the Star, which an army of expert electricians caused to flash and flame. The entrapment of Ben-Hur by Messala on the terrace of the Palace. The dim, enormous interior of the Roman Trireme. The wreck, and the struggle on machine-tossed "waves." The meeting of Ben-Hur, Esther, and Simonides (Henry Lee). The sunlit Grove of Daphne, with its grand temple of Apollo and *hundreds* of Roman maidens dancing in the festival. The Fountain of Castalia, fringed with towering palms; a lake shimmering in pale moonlight, gliding gondolas, Ben-Hur and the wily Iras (Corona Ricardo). The Sheik (Emmett Corrigan) and his tent. The oriental Orchard. The strident bettors at the arena. The cataclysmic race—two actual chariots;, each drawn by four real

Arabian horses lunging under the lash, wheels rumbling and swaying, now one, now the other vehicle ahead, until the incredible collision and Ben-Hur's triumph. The Palace again. Tirzah (Adeline Adler) and her mother (Mabel Bert) at the tomb of the lepers. The light and the miracle at Mount Olivet. The family reunion amid hymns.

The chariot race—a scene all action, with hardly a spoken word; the treadmills made such a racket that the actors' shouts could hardly be heard—brought down the house. "Wilder enthusiasm than that which followed this scene," reported the *World*, "has seldom manifested itself in a theatre." There were curtain calls after curtain calls—pandemonium.

Wallace looked straight ahead, apparently quite unmoved, until Mrs. Wallace touched him with her fan and whispered a few words. Erlanger led him to the stage, where he thanked the audience and begged to be excused from making a speech. The play went on to its conclusion, three hours and twenty-nine minutes after the curtain's rise. Wallace congratulated the steely-eyed Hart and wrote out statements for the *World* and *Herald* expressing satisfaction with the production. Wallace was particularly gratified at the tact and sensitiveness in the religious episodes.

From the beginning no one recorded a doubt that the play would be a popular success. Likewise the metropolitan critics were unanimous in asserting that it was not drama, but a kind of circus. (McKee, pp. 177-9).

Of course, there was lots of criticism from the elite, but the only critics who really counted, voted with their feet: they kept coming, and coming, and *coming*. People were entranced by the magnificent stage sets, costuming, lighting, music, but most of all by the chariot race. Nothing on this scale had ever been attempted before. Initially, performances were filled with New Yorkers, but after awhile, they began flooding in from elsewhere.

Wallace, the visionary dreamer with a flair for the dramatic, had written for the stage better than he knew. The play would go on to be performed an incredible 6,000 times—mostly in big cities and at hefty prices. Over a period of 21 years—with enlarged stages, many changes in actors, SRO signs, and full-length seasons --, it would draw over 20,000,000 people (America's total population was only 79,900,000 when the play opened!). Its record is unequaled in the history of theater.

1889 - 1900 --   It stayed in New York.
1900 - 1901 --   Besides New York, it also played in Philadelphia and Boston.
    Wallace testified that "Bill Farnum acts Ben-Hur as if he *were* Ben-Hur," and even though Farnum would go on to other things and many others assume the role, he would always remain, to his time, *THE* Ben-Hur. In Boston, the demand—mobs of people thronged the street—was so great that every seat was sold out in 15 minutes. During this period, Klaw and Erlanger, and Harper had collaborated on two big publishing ventures: Harper with its magnificent "Players Edition" (with 50 photographs and illustrations of the actors and action) and an elaborate horizontal souvenir album; complete with larger illustrations (and tissue separation sheets) of those same photographs and illustrations. These continued to be sold by the thousands.

Boston earned its place in drama history in that, by some fluke, Messala edged out Ben-Hur and won one of the chariot races there. William Hart chuckled about *that* the rest of his life.

1901 - 1902 -- It also played in Chicago, St. Louis, Pittsburgh, Philadelphia, Washington, D.C., Baltimore, Boston --, and overseas in London and Sydney, Australia.

Success now necessitated a third chariot in that heart-stopping race. An English company (led by Tearle and Medford) took the play to Sydney, Australia; and yet a third company (led by Taber and Gill) opened at Drury Lane, London. Among those there were Arthur Conan Doyle, Marie Tempest, and Sir Henry Irving. Within two weeks, British drama critics acknowledged that it was already the greatest success in the history of the foreign stage. Later, even King Edward and Queen Alexandra came to see it.

1902 - 1903 -- Now it was that finally the hinterland of America began to have the opportunity to see it. Crowds were so great, special trains had to be run. While religious thought-leaders like Campbell Morgan, popular British evangelist, might denounce the play and label it "blasphemous," to the tens of thousands who continued to flood the theaters, the experience was a profoundly moving one, and in that overwhelming last act, when the shaft of light blinded them with its radiance, tears ran down their faces and they felt they were in the presence of God.

1903 - 1904 -- The list of cities continued to expand, now including western cities as well. Now, trolley and other transportation lines began featuring huge *Ben-Hur* posters. Woodruff and Mackay's London company opened at the New York theater with *four* chariots!

1904 - 1905 -- The race took place to increase crowds at the St. Louis World Fair. William Farnum, having made his name a household word, left the cast for other dramatic ventures.

1905 - 1906 -- At Lincoln, Nebraska, the house caught fire during Act III. The performance went on in spite of it, with even more spectacular effects. In Rochester, police reserves had to be called in, to help control the unprecedented crowds.

1906 - 1907 -- More cities in Canada—such as Hamilton, Ottawa, and Montreal were added. There were now *five* chariots. Klaw and Erlanger presented a copy of *Ben-Hur* to every woman attending the 2,500th performance at the New York Academy of Music.

1907 - 1909 -- By now, Barnum and Bailey were in competition, with their own Ben-Hur chariot races!

1909-1913 -- By the fall of 1912, *Ben-Hur* was being played simultaneously on three continents.

1913 - 1915 -- Attendance records were broken at the San Francisco World Fair.

1914 - 1918 -- World War I most certainly curtailed the numbers of those who would otherwise have seen it. Billy Sunday declared that he wished 100,000,000 people, the entire nation, could see the play. William Jennings Bryan, that silver-tongued orator, publicly stated that "I have enjoyed *Ben-Hur* as the greatest play on the stage when measured by its religious tone and moral effect."

"Monk," a horse in the chariot scene, stayed with it for the entire 21-year run!

HIS FACE SUFFUSED, HIS EYES GLEAMING, ALONG THE REINS HE SEEMED TO FLASH HIS WILL

In 1918, the play closed—mainly because of the world-wide influenza epidemic that killed over 30,000,000 people, rivaling the death count of the entire "Great War" itself.

In 1920, it was performed again—and then closed (Klaw and Erlanger had terminated their thirty-year partnership) in the last week of April, in order to give the producers of the movie the entire field.

Actually, movie producers had already entered the lists. According to McKee, during the first sixty years of the book's history, it would have been almost impossible for anyone not to have heard about it. And those 20,000,000 who actually experienced it . . . well,

> almost without exception they cherished the chariot race until their dying day. "No church entertainment was complete," Hammond Lamont recalled, "unless the local amateur elocutionist let himself go in the chariot race; nobody who went to Sunday school could have escaped the story if he tried" (and Lamont could have omitted the "Sunday"). The nation sang Kelley's choruses, John H. Cody's "Ben-Hur March," E. T. Paul's "Tirzah's Serenade" and "Chariot Race"; at least fifteen other such popular songs circulated. Children, villages, and commercial products were named after Ben-Hur, Chariot races became a part of American life—not plain chariot races, but "Ben-Hur chariot races."
>
> Klaw and Erlanger made millions, Harpers and Wallaces hundreds of thousands, and a vast throng of actors, managers, stagehands, book-sellers, and other middlemen fattened on *Ben-Hur*. Some were happy because they received so much; some were bitter because they got no more.
>
> The ultimate canonization, of course, was bestowed by the movies. Late in 1907, Kalem (a pioneering group of producers—George Kleine, Samuel Long, and Frank Marion)

projected *Ben-Hur* in one reel, advertised as "positively the most superb moving picture spectacle ever made in America." The sixteen "magnificent" scenes had been filmed at Pain's Fireworks Show, Manhattan Beach, with costumes rented from the Metropolitan Opera House; the chariot race was performed by the "3rd Battery, Brooklyn," with Herman Rottjer as Ben-Hur. This version attracted some attention, until the producers were sued by Henry Wallace. It was the first time the infant industry had been seriously challenged in a copyright action. Stoutly defended by Kalem, the suit was fought through to the Supreme Court. Kalem argued that the movie was "merely a series of photographs," that it served as a good advertisement of the book and the stage play. But the final verdict, in 1910, went against the moviemen, who had to pay $25,000 in damages. *Ben-Hur* thus became the most costly one-reel scenario in cinema history. More significantly, it vindicated the legal rights of authors in a new and extensive field.

The closing of the play in 1920 was the signal for prolonged litigation to determine who actually owned the film rights. In 1921 Erlanger, Ziegfeld, and Charles B. Dillingham paid Henry Wallace $1,000,000 for them, according to the New York *Times*. Metro-Goldwyn-Mayer outbid other concerns in a resale, and labored for three years, 1922 - 1925, from Rome to Hollywood, expending $4,000,000 more on a scenario written by Carey Wilson and Bess Meredyth. The sea fight was enacted in the Mediterranean with fourteen vessels and twenty-eight hundred men. Ten thousand actors, one hundred and ninety-eight horses, a specially constructed grandstand three thousand feet long, forty-two cameras (one of them in an airplane) were necessary for the chariot race, which cost a quarter of a million. The premiere, long heralded, took place at the George M. Cohan Theater in New York, December 30, 1925. The cast for this, the "colossal" of "colossals," was a veritable constellation: Ramon Navarro as Ben-Hur; Claire MacDowell, his mother; Francis X. Bushman, Messala; May MacAvoy, Esther; Kathleen Myers, Iras; Hobart Bosworth, Arrius; Betty Bronson, the Madonna. The Bible scenes were in "natural" color.

The movie's first run on Broadway lasted twenty-two months, and then it pervaded the country and much of the world, after the manner of movies. Berlin applauded it; King George and Queen Mary attended a special showing at Windsor Castle; China banned it as pro-Christian propaganda. In 1931 it was revived, with sound effects. A movie edition of the novel sold enormously. Whosoever had not seen *Ben-Hur* before, saw it now, in cities, towns, hamlets. "*Ben-Hur* will be here—and continuously—until 1950," prophesied *Variety* in 1926.

"My God!" said Wallace to Edgar Kelley in 1899, when shown the *Ben-Hur* stage sets. "Did I set all this in motion?" He did not live to see half of what he had set in motion. Whether measured by the standards of literary criticism, or by the more impersonal statistics of copies and tickets sold, it was a stupendous achievement. (McKee, pp. 186-8).

But the version that most Americans today know is the 1959 MGM version, 212 minutes long, and in cinemascope color. It sported a huge cast, 300 sets, and exhausted all superlatives, virtually sweeping the Oscars in 1959 with eleven, and nominated for a twelfth. William Wyler and Sam Zimbalest were the guiding spirits and the principal actors included Charlton Heston, Jack Hawkins, Stephen Boyd, Haya Harareet, Hugh Griffith, and Sam Jaffe. Heston ran away with the film as Ben-Hur. And the 40-minute chariot race was anything but easy to film—in fact, one actor died in one of the crashes.

BIOGRAPHICAL SKETCH

"She will love me, and I shall make her famous by my pen and glorious by my sword.'

(Journal entry, July of 1847)

BEN-HUR TRIES THE HORSES

ONE

The Novitiate

Lewis Wallace was to be a dreamer, a romantic, an almost obsessed seeker after fame and fortune. A believer that anything is possible: all you have to do is, first dream it, then build foundations under that world, then make it happen.

The decisions of his life fall smoothly into four periods: (1) The Novitiate, (2) The Fair God, (3) Ben-Hur, and (4) The Prince—so that is the way this mini-bio will be structured.

The frontier was, from his earliest days, home. And he didn't have to look far to find success, for his father, "Colonel" David Wallace, variously President of the Senate, Lieutenant Governor, and Governor of the State of Indiana, was ever before him as a living testimony. And he was a West Point graduate as well; in fact, he taught there for several years before moving to the then just settling Brookville, Indiana. After studying law for a year with Judge Niles C. Eggleston, he was ready to pass the bar, then settle down with seventeen-year-old Esther French Test, daughter of a judge and sister of a judge-to-be. David, eleven years older than his bride, was a good-looking, serious, an intense young man, determined to succeed.

Four sons were born to the couple, in two-year-intervals (typical of the time): William in 1825, Lewis in 1827, John Test in 1829, and Edward Test in 1831. Esther was to bear the brunt of home responsibilities for David was always on the go, both with the Third Judicial Court and with the Assembly at Indianapolis. By 1832, the Colonel decided to move toward the Capital, settling in Covington on the Wabash River. On the way, the dreaded scarlet fever struck two of the boys: John died, but Lewis somehow made it through. Of this period, looking back, Wallace would write, "Of the sickness and death I recall two things distinctly—horrible draughts of saffron tea, hot almost to scalding, and the large brown eyes of my mother swimming in tears: (*Lew Wallace, An Autobiography*, p. 9.)

Indian attacks on the Covington settlement occurred from time-to-time. In fact, one of the boy's first images had to do with his father's drilling a group of militia in preparation for fighting Chief Black Hawk. War and fighting were not abstractions then, they were essential to survival itself.

At his paternal grandmother's knee, Lewis heard wonderful stories, stories of her uncle, John Paul Jones, and stories of her sitting on George Washington's knee. With her husband, Andrew, and eight children, they had moved from Cincinnati to Brookville.

> "Since that time I have seen many of the famous rivers of the earth, among them the Danube, the Rhine, and the Nile; never one of them impressed me as much as did the Wabash.... It looked so wide, so deep, so like the passing of a flood going down in its own majestic way to what would be a deluge when it at last arrived. Yet it had a coaxing power. My fears were soothed, and I went and, as it were, laid my hand on its mane; and thence we were friends. No one better than Dickens knew what conjurers such things are to imaginative children. I became its playmate the summers through." (*Autobiography,* p. 10).

And how the boy loved to fish! Nearby was a ferryman by the name of Nebeker. Lonely himself, he welcomed the little boy. Both listened intently for the sound of that horn: someone needed to cross over the river! His poor mother soon learned how often he was playing truant from school, and it certainly didn't take long to find out where he was; finally, she made a pact with the ferryman—and ceased worrying.

And what was he escaping from? A small one-room schoolhouse, with four windows and a door. At the front was the teacher—and hanging on the wall in clear view were the *rods*. Since truancy came ahead of lying and stealing in the man's catalogue of sins, poor Lewis was always getting thrashed. (His dear mother it was who taught him the alphabet and spelling). He and William each had a Webster spelling book, a paper slate, and a bluestone pencil. The latter, a little girl ate the first day of class. Not being able to produce it, Lewis got a flogging.

But Lewis's discovery that he could draw brought an entirely new dimension to his classroom struggles. But even that paled in comparison to the discovery that he could *read*! And *never* would he forget that first book.

> My first book! Ah, how distinctly it comes to me through the years! One of Peter Parley's. A Yankee lad ran away and went to sea, and in the Mediterranean was taken, ship and all, by Algerines. But he escaped. The vessel lay close under the guns of a fort. The prisoners were to be sold for slaves next morning. A shipmate, looking through a port, saw a small boat loose on the water. The squeeze through the port was trying, but they made it and the small boat. By good luck, the oars were there ready. Better still, the pirates kept no watch. The two rowed to sea, and, after suffering hunger and thirst, were picked up by Christians. How it made me shiver, that crisis when the lad, afraid to drop, hung to the edge of the narrow window, thinking of home and mother, and muttering the prayer she had taught him. Then the dark water closing over him—Goodness! Would he rise? Could he swim? I got the tale nearly by heart. The craving it awoke is not yet satisfied.

My mother, meantime, made discovery that to keep me in bounds there was nothing like a book. So she bethought her of a long, good one—*The Scottish Chiefs.*

I was a slow reader, and Miss Porter's pages lacked the charming simplicity of Mr. Goodrich's. There was halting and stumbling at first; the broad Scotch proper names refused to be spelled; but at length I reached the current of the story, and when it dawned upon me that it was about a man who was actually named after my brother William— it did not occur to me that my brother could have been named after him—astonishment and delight came to the help of my understanding, and bore it up and on as in the Arabian Nights friendly genii were wont to carry distressed princes through the air. Then my brother read the wondrous tale, and we debated it early and late. We cried over its sorrowful passages, trembled while the battles were in progress, and were genuine Scots whether the victory were for or against us, especially when the sword and directing genius of our mighty kinsman were in the least conspicuous. That he was our kinsman we had no doubt.

Was such pleasure to be bottled up for us alone? We called in our chums, one Robert Evans, and two others, Henderson Rawles and Wesley Harper. The five read the heroic chronicles together; whereupon we turned them into a play. Each took a character. On account of his name my brother's right to the role of Sir William was admitted. Evans took Robert Bruce; Rawles and Harper had their parts; and I was given the role of the youthful brother of the love-lorn Helen Mar. Then, in deadliest earnest, we went to war with the haughty English. We made helmets of paste-board and swords of seasoned clapboards. The young hazel-shoots we wove into shields. Our steeds we found ready in the bottom, and that they were of ironweeds did not detract from their fitness. Under us they had the endurance of Arabs and the strength of the big Flemings so affected by knights who ate, drank, and slept in steel. Neither did we see any inconsistency in converting the same weeds into lances. Thus armed and panoplied we ranged the country round. Woe to the elder, the mullen, and the white-crowned lobelias. Woe particularly to the wild sunflower cropping myriadly in the dry hollows under the trees along the river-bank. A vigorous growth of fruiting pokeberries was an enemy to be dealt with in single combat. The sword was then the preferred weapon. Out rode Sir William or the Bruce, and they always came back victorious, their blades dyed to the hilt, their shields dripping with gore. (*Autobiography,* pp. 20-22).

Then, at school, the volatile Irishman disappeared—whither no one seemed to know. In his place, when the school at last reopened, was a woman. A *woman!* And there were no rods hanging on the wall. Then she put into his hands two books:

> . . . an elementary arithmetic and an Olney's Geography. The first had a dismal look about it. Further investigation satisfied me that it and I could never be friends. I say *never,* and so it has proved. The other book captivated me at once. Turning its leaves, I was arrested by a display of maps and pictures. The horizon, theretofore bounding the village and its vicinity, seemed to undergo a swift and vast extension. I caught glimpses of other countries and peoples. The sea teemed with islands, and actually there were rivers larger than the Wabash. Most marvelous—incredible—impossible—the earth was round, like an apple. To catch a boy and hold him fast one had only to set the delicate machinery of the wonder-box in him at work. The suggestion is respectfully submitted to teachers. Mothers, with better understanding, practice it when lullabies fail. At all events, I became interested in the study, and to such a degree that through the years intervening nothing pertaining to geography has been allowed to escape me. With

Columbus and Magellan, La Pérouse, Cook, and Perry I still sail and sail. In more modern times, I volunteer under Franklin and Kane, and ingratiate myself hail-fellow-well-met with Livingstone and Stanley. The increase of knowledge due to their heroism has been practically an enlargement of the world; yet—I go back to the repetition knowingly—none of their discoveries has been so wonderful to me, so hard to reconcile with appearances, so defiant of problematic solution, as that the earth is not flat, like a pancake.

One of the wonders of childhood I have never seen satisfactorily explained is the greater length of the divisions of time in passage. A day then was like a month now, a month like a lifetime in fulness. And those summers! There was not a minute of them between sunrise which I did not devote to physical delights of some kind. So eager was I to be doing something with hands and feet—walking, running, swimming, hunting, exploring, playing—that shoes and hat and coat were alike abominations. Breakfast over, I was off for the day. If dinners had grown on the trees like bread-fruit in some of the Pacific islands, and the getting them had required the abandonment of an amusement, though for a time barely enough to pluck and eat them, they might as well not have been. Hunger did not seem to exhaust me, or rather in my mid-going I never thought of food. Malaria, the curse of the beautiful new country, attacked without stopping me. The rigor and the fever often struck me in the woods or water; I took them as matters of course and went on. . . .

Autumn, it is to be added, was but an extension of summer a little sobered, and different in that things ceased growing that they might ripen—a difference I saw and felt without understanding. I speak altogether of wild things—richness with which men had nothing to do. Who better than I knew where to look for the fattest hazel and hickory nuts, chincapins the least acrid, grapes in largest cluster, pawpaws the most melting?

... But alas for me when winter came and the universal green had vanished, and the snow lay over my haunts and even the river yielded itself to bonds hateful and icy! *That* was an end of going. And, in recognition of the distasteful fact, I submitted to hat, shoes, and coat, and became an *habitué* of the red school-house on the hill. There my penmanship improved. I could copy a copy with an identicalness really wonderful considering that we are bound to the use of quills not always clarified. True, the multiplication table continued a rough corduroy over a swamp of bottomless depth; yet my maps were unexcelled. In fact, had the one crowded room of the small building been better furnished, my progress might have been more satisfactory. As it was, in periods extremely cold, a struggle began with us the moment we were rapped to order. The fireplace was ample and wood in plenty, but the floors and windows were open; they and the big boys and girls monopolized the warmth. In the rush for the fire at recess, the small children were shut out unanimously. The wall of writhing bodies that cut them off could not be climbed, while the process of tunneling under was dangerous. Study requires favorable conditions. It may be questioned if the author of *Vathek* could have finished his marvelous story in the prescribed time if compelled to pause between sentences to blow the blood back in his frosting fingers. It is also beyond belief that *Nuova Vita* could have been conceived while zero was nibbling at Dante's toes.

I remember yet the wonder which fell upon the school and held it when, without notice, a party of men entered the room one bitter cold day and set a large iron box tenderly upon the floor; then fixed legs to it, and, after knocking a hole in the chimney above the fireplace, put up a long line of iron pipes in connection. Of all the urchin eyes watching the operation not one lost a motion while their rough but gentle friends kindled a fire in the box. And then, when the draught began to sing, and presently the warmth intensified and pervaded from the centre to the corners, and we *all alike* felt the summary effect. If the inventor of stoves had been of a nature purely Samaritan and conscious of silent blessings in the air about him that moment, doubloons in showers fresh from the Spanish mints had not been more to his satisfaction. It was my first encounter with a stove. (*Autobiography*, pp. 26-29).

At last, childhood, as he had known it, came to an end. His loving mother, the sun that started his day and the moon that ended it, succumbed to another of the great killers of the time—there were so many, and what few doctors there were knew so little. If you died, it was God's will; and if you survived, it was God's will, too. This particular killer they called consumption (similar to today's tuberculosis). Mother's was worse yet: *"galloping* consumption"—so named because of the speed at which it attacked. And here she was, with three little boys—9, 7, and 3. Who would take care of them when she was gone?

> Yet her eyes grew brighter and dwelt upon her boys with a gaze longer and more intense. Now I know why. She was thinking of the inevitable separation. My father was in New York on business, and dreamless of what was to occur. The sufferer wanted nothing possible to be had. One night I lay asleep before the fire upon a rug which I affected on account of the great Persian lion woven in it. One of the women in attendance shook me, saying, "Wake up—your mother is dying; come and see her." My elder brother was already at the bedside, crying bitterly. He knew the meaning of what was passing; I did not. In dull apprehension I joined him. The alabaster tinge was on her

face. In the eyes there was no light. The hands and tongue had lost their affectionate cunning. I called her, using the endearment that had never before failed—"Mother, mother!" She did not answer, and then I understood the silence. The comprehension fell upon me as darkness leaps in on the blowing-out of the last light, and it seemed a strong hand caught my heart and tried to wring the life out of it. And so I made acquaintance with death. I have seen it since in many forms, at times under circumstances hideous because of its accessories—in flood, in pestilence, in battle—but never realized its awful import, due, as I can now perceive, to an intuitive perception of the extent of the bereavement it so remorselessly inflicted on me. She was to be buried. I was never to see her more. Her love with all its countless illustrations of touch, look, care, sympathy, and word, was to become but a memory. In my defeats, how often I have said to myself, "Ah, if she were here to console me!" in triumphs, "How proud and happy she would be!" (*Autobiography*, pp. 33-4).

Wallace would spend the rest of his life looking for her, trying to conceptualize all that she was, asking about her . . . to people who knew her literally rather than as an authority figure. All he could remember were her large, sparkly, and deep brown eyes.

> They follow me yet. Indeed, through my seventy years there has never been a day so bright or a night so dark that, upon recurrence of the thought of them, I have been unable to see them seeing me. (*Autobiography*, p. 32).

Strangely enough, it was not from his father but from one of his mother's rejected suitors that he learned the most about his mother. Reminiscing many years later, with Wallace, certain things stood out:

> Sprightliness, beauty, and graces of person, he said, brought her beaus in numbers. She was an instance, he further observed, in which coquetry added to a character altogether perfect. He spoke of her as the strangest compound he ever met. Though delicate to frailty, she could dance from Sunday to Sunday. A Methodist, charitable as a Sister of Mercy, devout as a Puritan, the enjoyment she found in the party and the ball, in visitation and in society, were irrepressible. I may remark that at the time he was speaking the suitor was old and semi-paralytic; still, he made it clear to me that the subject of his speech was the unforgotten brightest light on the receding hill-top of his youth. (*Autobiography*, p. 32).

Almost half a century later, he would name his greatest heroine after his mother.

A kind neighbor, Mrs. John Hawkins, after the funeral, took the three homeless children home with her, and cared for them as if they were her own. The next several years, he spent pretty much as before: summers in the woods and along the river; winters, sledding and trapping birds; school he endured as best he could, and escaped often. When his beloved elder brother William was sent away to school, Lewis ran away to attend Wabash College with him. He was there two months before he left on his own.

One day, William met him at his boarding house. He had news.

> "Come," he said, "make haste and wash yourself, and put on some clean clothes."
>
> "Why, what's the matter?" I asked.

"Father's at the tavern, and he has brought us a—" He hesitated.

"A what?" said I.

"A new mother."

All the rebellious sparks in my nature blew together and broke into a flame.

"Well, she may be your mother, but she's not mine. I'll not go. Who is she?" (*Autobiography*, p. 45).

Towards the end of his second term as Lieutenant governor, Col. Wallace had met Zerelda G. Sanders, eldest daughter of Dr. John H. Sanders, a wealthy physician. There was some family opposition, but Zerelda had a mind of her own: on December 26, 1836, she met the groom at a hotel and married him. After the legislative session concluded, the Governor-to-be moved back to Crawfordsville with his new wife; the three boys were gathered in—and there was a home once again.

The poor woman had anything but an easy time with Lewis. First of all, they were living in a public house rather than private residence. Although she gave him every attention, he was sulky and stubborn; he refused to have anything to do with her, went truant again, spending much of his time in the woods and creek. His *real* mother was buried there in the lonely Covington graveyard: "*She* was my mother, and I would have no other—I would die sooner." But the new stepmother quietly bided her time, waiting to be needed. It came:

> One evening I returned from two days of truancy, nearly dead of croup. She put me to bed, and nursed me with infinite skill and tenderness. I had sense enough to know she

was the savior of my life, and called her mother; and in speech and fact mother she has been to me ever since. (*Autobiography*, p. 46).

Now began a new life, and with the 1837 election to the governorship, the family moved to Indianapolis, and there in a convenient, though plain, dwelling, they settled down.

This transfer was to me like being set down in a new world. Indianapolis was, in fact, scarcely emerged from the woods. Stumps were frequent in its vacant downtown lots, and wagons stalled on its main streets; nevertheless, the "Capital' had all the effect upon me of a great metropolis. The overwhelming sense with which I beheld the state-house, then recently finished, and gala in its fresh stucco, serves me now as a ready measure of my verdancy and inexperience. What a marvelous achievement it appeared within and without! And when, in fulfilment of years of patient dreaming, I at last stood under the portico of the Acropolis at Athens, its pillars, with all their height and hugeness of diameter, affected me less than did those of the cheap imitation of which I am writing. Where the Soldiers' Monument stands there was then a pretentious quadrangular brick building designed originally as a residence for the governors of the commonwealth, but about as unfit for the purpose as a painted balloon; indeed, there was never wife of a governor so foolish as to wish to try living in it; withal, however, the Versailles of one of the most extravagant of the French kings was not nearly the palace I saw in that red habitation of rats, bats, and twittering swallows. Verily, the creative in the imagination of a man, even though he be a poet, is not a tithe part of that in the eyes of a boy. (*Autobiography*, pp. 47-8).

Gradually, life settled down, and, no small thanks to his new mother, he became less of a wild child and more of a clean, well-combed, civilized one. And on Sundays, she insisted that her boys attend church with her. Church wasn't so bad, not if he could draw people around him.

Mr. Jacob Cox was the premier painter of the capital city, and Lewis decided he'd become an artist, too. Art became his new obsession—this, too, at the cost of school attendance. That is, until his father called him into his study one day and told him he would have to give up his drawing.

When he began to bow his back, his father, knowing him well, struck at ihs son's most vulnerable point: "I suppose you don't want to be a poor artist—poor in the sense of inability as well as poverty. To be a great painter, two things have always been necessary—a people of cultivated taste and then education for the man himself. You have neither." (*Autobiography*, pp. 50, 51).

School remained the same. The teacher was subject to blind rages. One recess, he caught Lewis sketching on the blackboard—sketching the teacher's head on a rabbit. That afternoon, he called the artist to the front of the room and beat him until the blood ran down his bare legs.

That did it. He gave up the dream of becoming a great artist—but not without lifelong regret: "Still it haunts me. At this day even, I cannot look at a great picture without envying its creator the delight he must have had while it was in evolution. And, why not make the confession unreservedly? Why not admit that in biographical literature there are no lives so fascinating and zestful to me as those of master-artists?" (*Autobiography*, p. 52).

So, he turned back to the printed page. In the State-house was a library. He decided to explore—not knowing that day would dramatically change his life.

> There was a suggestion of stealth in the stillness of my steps on the carpeted floor. From having been in the British Museum and the Vatican, I now know how small the

total of the collection of books was; at that time, however, I had never imagined such a presence of volumes *en masse*. The observation was from a central position. Slowly, very slowly, I swept the four sides, lined with shelving to a height out of reach except with the aid of a ladder. Books everywhere, of all sizes, of all colors! Had any one ever read them all? Of the cumulative labor required for their production, and the *mind* in them, I did not think, any more than I thought of the motive, that deepest abstraction underlying each of them—they were revelations time was to bring me.

Presently an itching of the fingers, like that which caught me when grinding colors for my friend the artist, seized me; only, in this instance, it went not further than an intense desire to handle separately every book in the array, exactly as one boy always wants to feel the pocket-knife and marbles he sees in the hands of another boy. There was a step-ladder, the property of the librarian, and he being out—it would have mattered nothing had he been present—I carried it into a corner and set about prospecting the shelves. Noon came, and I was still at work. Thinking, doubtless, that my father was a colleague of his in the government of the state, and that so much comity might not be unsafe, the keeper let me have my bent. I forgot I was due at school, and that dinner was a due of mine. Closing hour in the evening arrived; then I gave up to return next day—and the next—and next—until the review was done. At the end, I had located every picture-book in the heap, even as a sportsman marks his fallen birds.

The last remark, I perceive, is open to an inference that none but the picture-books interested me. But the incident is not concluded—far from it. In the overhaul I came upon a volume entitled *Astoria*, and another, *The Last of the Mohicans*. Let say to the contrary who will, there is something in names. These attracted me, and in good time I went back to them, with result that I uncovered one of the most continuous, if not the greatest, happiness which had befallen me. In the most impressional period of my life I was introduced to Washington Irving and Fenimore Cooper, or, more plainly, to their works; and I revelled in them, especially Cooper's, whose subjects were better adapted to my opening mind. For months and months after that discovery my name figured on the receipt register of the library more frequently than any other. I took the treasures, now a sea story, now a Leatherstocking Tale, and, in the haymow or off alone in the woods, sailed and sailed with the Red Rover, or, from the store of quaint old Natty Bumpo, eked my fill of wisdom. My rating at school was the worst; yet, strange to say, education went on with me, for I was acquiring a habit of reading. Looking back to the thrashings I took stoically and without a whimper, I console myself thinking of the successful lives there have been with not a jot of algebra in them. (*Autobiography*, pp. 53-4).

For his thirteenth year, his father sent him to a teacher in Centreville, hoping that he might motivate where so many others had not. Since an aunt lived in the town, supposedly she would look after him once in a while and keep him from running wild. William was there as further influence. Professor Hoshour proved to be all the Governor hoped he would be. Looking back at the experience many years later, Wallace described the man and his methodology.

> Professor Samuel K. Hoshour—his name is purposely given in full—came more nearly to my ideal school-master than any to whose tender mercies it had been my lot to fall. He wielded the rod and vigorously, but with discrimination and undeniable justice, and really taught me. He even interested me in arithmetic. Getting me to his house of evenings, with infinite patience he would cipher me over

the knottier problems, explaining the rules pencil in hand. Better evidence of Christian nature no man can furnish.

Professor Hoshour was the first to observe a glimmer of writing capacity in me. An indifferent teacher would have allowed the discovery to pass without account; but he set about making the most of it, and in his method there was so much wisdom that it were wrong not to give it with particularity, the more so as some modern pedagogue may in that way be helped to an understanding of what I mean by discrimination applied to pupils.

The general principle on which the professor acted is plain to me now. The lack of aptitude for mathematics in my case was too decided not to be apparent to him; instead of beating me for it, he humanely applied himself to cultivating a faculty he thought within my powers and to my taste. Or, in another form, poverty of talent in one line, as he reasoned, might be compensated for by the development of ability in another.

I remember his beginning perfectly; inasmuch as it set me to wondering that one could waste time and effort in plying a lad like me with a subject so serious and seemingly beyond my years. What had he on which to believe that I could even understand what he said to me? But when at length I saw I could understand him, and that he too saw it, how delicious the flattery! And what stimulation there was in it!

. . . .

I recall also a saying of the professor's own.

"Were you to ask me," he said, "which of the rules is the most important, which comes nearest being the essence of the whole art, here it is: In writing, everything is to be sacrificed to clearness of expression—everything."

By way of illustration, I suppose, he next produced a volume which he called *The Spectator*.

"Here," he said, "are some of the finest examples of clear English ever printed. I will select some of the best. Now listen." He read a paragraph, and declared, "You can't help understanding that."

. . . .

Taking a New Testament, "There," he said, "read that. It is the story of the birth of Jesus Christ."

This was entirely new to me, and I recall the impression made by the small part given to the three wise men. Little did I dream then what those few verses were to bring me—that out of them *Ben-Hur* was one day to be evoked.

I can see the professor standing in his door, lamp in hand and bareheaded, dismissing me for the night, with exactly the same civilities he would have sped an official the most important in the state. Ah, the kindly cunning of the shrewd old gentleman! He had dropped a light into my understanding and caught me.

So, step by step, the professor led me into and out of depths I had never dreamed of, and through tangles of subtlety and appreciations which proved his mind as thoroughly as they tried mine. Before the year was out he had, as it were, taken my hand in his and introduced me to Byron, Shakespeare, and old Isaiah. The year was the turning-point of my life, and out of my age and across his grave I send him, Gentle master, hail, and all sweet rest! Now I know wherein I am most obliged to you—unconsciously, perhaps, but certainly you taught me how to educate myself up to every practical need. (*Autobiography*, pp. 56-59).

So it came to pass that he took up his pen and began writing; he wrote things like historical poems in the style of "Marmion" and "Lay of the Last Minisrel"; an epic poem titled "Travels of a Bed-bug" which proved to hit too close to home for it was a thinly-veiled expose of a prominent Indianapolis lawyer. Things were rather uncomfortable for him in Indiana's capital city for some time after he let it loose.

Next came his first novel: *The Man-at Arms: A Tale of the Tenth Century*; and he started out on the wrong foot by naming it before he really knew what it was about. It was melodramatic, bloody, thunderous, stereotypical, romantic, and more than a bit amateurish. Nevertheless, young Lewis put a *lot* of time and effort into the 250-page manuscript, and ever after regretted its destruction while he was away from home. At least he could have laughed at it in years to come. But it *did* season his literary timbers, giving him writing experience that would stand him in good stead during the years to come.

There is an old folk saying that is apropos here: "The apple never falls far from the tree." And another equally appropriate one: "You never really value anything until you fear it may be lost." Like most teenagers, Lewis took his home, his parents, his security, pretty much for granted. Several times, he had attempted to run off on this adventure or another. School, he never took seriously; rather, he lived in his own dream world of books and the stories he created himself. Ambivalently, he wanted to soar into the heavens, yet who would really want to leave the comforts of home?

His father decided it for him.

Lewis would always remember that day as a day apart: a dividing line between his childhood and the rest of his life. In recent weeks, he had more than once caught his father watching him—intently, with a serious brooding look in his eyes.

> Calling me into the library one morning after breakfast, he told me he had something to say. From the drawer of a table supporting the bookcase he drew a package of papers neatly folded and tied with red tape. Seldom have I seen him so deliberate and serious.
>
> "I want you to look at the papers in this package," he said.
>
> I returned the parcel.
> "What are they?" he asked.
>
> "Receipts."
>
> "Receipts for what?"
>
> "I take them to be receipted school-bills."
>
> "Were I to die to-night," he continued, "your portion of my estate would not keep you a month. I have struggled to give you and your brothers what, in my opinion, is better than money—education. Since your sixth year I have paid school-bills for you; but—one day you will regret the opportunities you have wilfully thrown away. I am sorry, disappointed, mortified; so, without shutting the door upon you, I am resolved that from to-day you must go out and earn your own livelihood. I shall watch your course hopefully. That is all I have to say."
>
> He waited to hear from me, and, as he was standing, I brought him a chair.

The announcement did not surprise me. Indeed, it had frequently occurred to me to ask him for permission to do the thing he now laid upon me. What I could resort to had been considered. As it was, he had not cast me off, but simply left me to myself—that saved my self-love. I admitted the justice of his course. I admitted also the duty he owed the younger children, my half-brother and his sister, and ended by thanking him for all his kindness to me in the past. That I could take care of myself was not to be doubted.

At the close of the interview he said, "Had you not better keep the receipts?"

"Why should I keep them?"

"Some time," he returned, "you may be disposed to think I have not done a whole part by you; should that happen, you have only to turn to this package and count the years it covers."

I assured him I needed no reminder.

Only a skeleton of a conversation is given. There was no argument, no reproach, no entreaty. The affair was merely as if one party were making the other a present; and such in fact it was—he had given me my freedom. His affection stood demonstrated. He had punished me often and severely, but never undeservedly. He was a good man and patient; I had been a bad boy—that was all. Life was before me in which to make him amends. Had I been less confident of earning my bread respectably, my feelings might have worn a different color. He offered me his hand. I took it, and passed out of the house and into the street rather lightsomely.
At the gate in going I remember stopping to look back at the house; and I see it yet made more lasting in recollection

by my father standing in the open door under the low portico. It will not be hard to understand what brought and held him there while I remained in sight.

. . . .

What made the humble home so dear to me that when I think of it now I feel a softening of the tear-ducts and a hardening in the throat?

Father, mother—the time had long gone since I refused the word to her who had so wisely replaced my mother in fact—brothers of the old family and brother and sister of the new had dwelt there with me. Still, that is not wholly satisfying. To find the perfect answer, I have to go deep. Here it is, nothing simpler when at last reached—it was the life of daily passage under that roof.

The housekeeping had been exquisite, the hours easy and natural, and without hectoring or scolding. We had known but one despotic law—that we should be present and ready for meals. Often as it pleased us, we had attended church. Every nook and cranny had been free to us.

. . . .

But of all that went to make pleasant life there nothing returns to me so delightfully as my father's part. I have spoken of his love for literature. It was little short of a passion, and he stinted himself in many ways to gratify it. He was a subscriber to all the great British quarterly magazines, and bought the best editions of the best books. The efforts he made to impart his feelings for them to us were untiring. Of contemporary writers, Macaulay commanded his highest admiration. The *Essays*, he declared, were the perfection of English. The impatience with which he awaited the arrival of the *Edinburgh Review* was undisguised; and if the number, at last to hand, contained a paper of Macaulay's, he plunged into it as a hungry child falls to over a bowl of bread-and-milk. Finished, then came one of what we called his readings.

In the summer those readings were given irregularly. They were rather sovereign graces reserved for winter evenings, and then he was accustomed to favor us two or three times a week. We prepared for them. One of us brought in the wood and piled it against the foot of the mantel in the sitting-room. The fireplace was broad and high, and the hearth a real old-fashioned, pioneer hearth. Except as it has been perpetuated in verse and story, its like is vanishing, if not entirely lost. Beginning with the laying of the back-log, the making the fire was an art calling for skill; then, in its initial state of smoke and crackle, the table was rolled forward, the lamp adjusted, and the easy-chair put in place. What matter if outside the snow grizzled the world or the wind blew distempered down to zero? Presently the blaze broke out, the hearth reddened, a new light leaped along the low ceiling and over the curtains of the bed in the corner, and summer shut the doors against the uninvited winter at its back. We were ready; so was the reader.

My father had a face complementary of a beautiful head. A more serviceable voice for the carriage of delicate feeling I never heard. It was of all the middle tones, and remarkably sensitive to the touch of the thought to be rendered. Rather weak for denunciation, in pathetic passages it was like a master ballad-singer's. The featuring and eye-rolling, the mouthing and falsetto tricks of the professional recitationist he abhorred, saying they were unnatural and distractive. I have heard three men whose faces in animated speech suffused with glow suggestive of transfiguration—S. S. Prentiss, Edward A. Hannegan, and David Wallace.

It should not be inferred that in his readings my father confined himself to Macaulay; he gave us the choicest of everything, though, as with all who find pleasure in general literature, he had his favorites. He delighted, for example, in the *Essays of Elia;* Shakespeare and Milton he regarded with a kind of awe. It was from him I first had the full effects of "The Lay of the Last Minstrel' and "Childe Harold." He fixed my standard of pulpit eloquence by the sermons of Dr. Chalmers, Robert Hall, Bossuet, and Bourdaloue. Once he gave an evening to Thucydides, and so powerful was his rendition of the retreat of the Athenians from Syracuse that it has since been one of my exemplars in historical writing. Nor have I yet lost the impression he made on me by Bancroft's exquisite story of the Jesuits in New France. In a word, by his reading he relieved every masterly production to which he addressed himself of heaviness, or, rather, he brought it down to my perfect comprehension.

These readings, it should be further said, did not always occupy the whole of the evenings. My brother and I were frequently required to take the floor and conclude them with declamations. The method pursued at such times permitted us to go through our respective exercises once without interruption and as best we could; after which we were subjected to criticisms covering every part of each performance from the first to the last bow. Of the parts, in our father's opinion, particularly objectionable, repetitions were had until they often ran into laborious drilling. His most peremptory requirement was that we should speak every word distinctly. A man might be awkward in manner, he argued, careless in dress, homely in feature, false in premise, illogical, even ungrammatical, yet a good speaker, if he only enunciated clearly, and was in earnest.

The paternal law allowed us to select the pieces in which we were to appear. If they were unfamiliar to the grave president, he called for the book and held it on us; if we halted in the delivery, he turned us down summarily. On such occasions the audience was privileged to laugh at our discomfiture. Ere long we got beyond "Hohenlinden" and "Marco Bozzaris," and, growing ambitious, advanced to longer themes; such as, in prose, extracts from Webster, Emmet's "Vindication," Phillips's "Washington"; in poetry, Collins's "Ode to the Passions," Byron's "Corsair," Scott's "Marmion" and the "Battle of Beal-un-duine."

I dwell on these things to make it easy to see what life was in the old homestead, and that it was not merely well-regulated and comfortable in the creature point of view, but had an educational side as well. So, too, a stranger will better understand how much I was losing now that I was to cut loose and take care of myself; that, besides the loss of home in the purest sense of the term, I was abandoning the oversight and care of a preceptor whose capacity to instruct was quickened marvelously by his natural affection. What were the new associations awaiting me? Out of the gate into the street, never to return except as a guest! I very much fear there was lacking in me the proper appreciation of the solemnity and uncertainties of the crises. (*Autobiography*, pp. 78-84).

BEN-HUR AND ILDERIM

TWO

The Fair God

So . . . he was on his own—at sixteen. His formal education had not had much of an impact—but, such as it was, it was now over. His informal education had only begun. It would take many years for him to sort everything out. In 1887, he would note, "My education, such as it was, is due to my father's library." Equally much a part of his education had been watching and listening to his father: his unfailing courtesy and respect for others, his carriage, his drive, his presence—he was a prince among men.

But introspection comes only with time—now he must earn a living somehow; decide just what he wanted to do in life. It would be a long twisting road, punctuated with many a comma, ellipsis, colon, semi-colon, question mark, exclamation mark along the way toward the eventual period. Many side-roads, many rabbit trails that seemingly led nowhere—but, in the eternal scheme of things, each a necessary part of the overall journey.

First of all, he would work in the office of Robert B. Duncan, the County Clerk, copying documents at ten cents per hundred words; this job would provide food and lodging for his body. The state library, he continued to raid. In his father's library he had first come across Prescott's monumental three-volume work, *The Conquest of Mexico.* It had *everything!* " . . . how delightful it was! . . . as a tale, how rich in attractive elements—adventure, exploration, combat, heroisms, oppositions of fate and fortune, characters for sympathy, characters for detestation, civilization and religion in mortal combat." (McKee, p. 10).

Out of all this, and out of the sophomoric ashes of *The Man-of-Arms*, would rise *The Fair God*, his first published book. But the road would be a long one—thirty long years—before it would be ready. Meanwhile, he would begin by re-reading Prescott, learning Spanish, and, then wading into the likes of Bernal Diaz, Torquemada, Hervara, Sahagun, and others. It began in a blank book one cold winter evening. There was then no inkling that it would result in anything more than an exercise in passing the time. The thirty years that followed would be years of action, years of treading an epic stage, years of making decisions that changed the course of history. But wherever he went, the story would go with him, and grow, intersticed in slivers of silence and inaction. In long marches, in tense watches, in trains and stations, thoughts would come unexpectedly, and be written down . . . and the tree would grow—a twig at a time. Its timber would season in the storms that assailed him. Thousands would fall at his side—tens of thousands, *hundreds* of thousands—but he would be spared. A Higher Power than he willed it so.

First of all, if the book were to be real . . . the setting must be real. "Manifest Destiny," the mantra which glorified even the basest motives, waved high over the America of the 1840's. It was God's will that the American flag wave from sea to sea. Whatever was in the way must be taken out, no questions asked. Indians were in the way—they must be broken, tamed, and reservationized. French, British, and Russians were in the way—they must be defeated or bought off. But most in the way were the Spanish and Mexicans.

The French were already taken care of: Jefferson's purchase of that third of the nation had taken place forty years before, in 1803. That left England and Russia in the northwest and vast Mexico in the southwest. The Viceroyalty of New Spain had once stretched from the Oregon Territory to Panama, from California to Florida, from Baja to Trinidad. We had taken Florida in 1819, but Mexico, inheritor of most of Spain's great viceroyalty, stood still—huge and defiant—blocking our way. It still stretched from California to Louisiana, and north to Kansas, Colorado, and Oregon.

All this young Lew sensed, for he was ever attuned to his time. Although he didn't yet know what he wanted to do with his life, he did know that he yearned for glory—and that pathway, he knew, would most likely be bloodied by the sword. Down on the southern border, General Zachary Taylor was casting lusting eyes south and west, determined, by hook or crook, to mess up Mexico and thereby batter his way west. A huge gouge had already been chomped out of hapless Mexico by Sam Houston and his Texas patriots. By March of 1846, Taylor had advanced to Matamoros on the Rio Grande. Enough provocation occurred to justify a state of emergency; in May, Congress declared that "by the act of the Republic of Mexico, a state of war between that Government and the United States existed"—and 50,000 troops were called for.

Many miles to the north, nineteen-year-old Lew Wallace was studying law, preparing for the bar exam. But his heart was south: what if war should come and go—and no glory come to him? Thanks to *The Fair God*, Mexico was ever in his thoughts—even without old Zach Taylor down on the borders; "It was like the attendant of the Aztec King, in service to amuse and entertain his master. In the car, at way-stations, of evenings here and there, in breaks of business, I had only to take paper and pencil and my entertainment was ready. In anticipation of such opportunities, it grew a habit with me after a while to carry scraps of paper in my pocket to receive such jottings as appeared worthy a place in the manuscript; or, wanting them, I utilized envelopes and blank spaces in letters for the purpose. A singular faculty was the outgrowth. The last writing might have ended in the middle of a sentence, yet weeks after, whether on the street or in an assemblage, I could begin where the stop occurred and go on exactly as if the manuscript were before me." (*Autobiography*, p. 91).

The manuscript had continued to grow—and with it, so did the writer:

> "Montezuma, Guatamozin, Mualox, Hualpa, and Tecetl had admitted me to intimacy; and on the sea, much more than were clairvoyant spectres, Cortés and his *cidelantados* passed the time not devoted to their steeds watching the Tabascan coast and speculating upon the mines and *haciendos* awaiting them in the vast perspective of the unknown called Mexico.
>
> "Now, too, more distinctly than ever, I felt the impulses of manhood in near approach. The ego in me began its wrestle with the question, probably the most serious of life to every one not in condition to exist without labor—what am I to do with myself? A fine speech, a bit of good writing, something brave read of in the world of action, had often a disturbing effect; and then, were I in the vault, work upon the record under hand turned into a process like nothing I could think of so much as pouring precious wine into a rathole. In the years to come, who would ask for the book or for the clerk whose days it had converted? Was I to be always a copyist?" (*Autobiography*, pp. 97-98).

Even before Wallace took his bar examination, he knew he'd be heading to Mexico. In fact, so full had his head been with Mexico that he had studied hardly at all for the exam. When he finished, he wrote the Examining Judge a note:

> "Dear Sir,—I hope the foregoing answers will be to your satisfaction more than they are to mine; whether they are or not, I shall go to Mexico.
> "Respectfully, Lew Wallace."
> If the judge were wanting an excuse to punish me, I had furnished it. Two or three days afterwards I received a notice through the post-office:
>
> "Supreme Court-Room, Indianapolis.
> "Mr. Lew Wallace:
> "Dear Sir,—The Court interposes no objection to your going to Mexico.
> "Respectfully,
> "Isaac Blackford."
>
> The communication was unaccompanied with a license. (*Autobiography*, pp. 112-113).

In order to go to Mexico, there had to be a company to join, so Wallace organized one. After advertising, within three days the company was full. A big crowd was there to see them off. Thousands shook their hands, sensing many of these young men, leaving so joyously, would never return. As they marched towards the wagons that would carry them to the train connection in Edinburg, his father marched with him.

> At my side, keeping step with me, he trudged along through the dust. The moment came for me to climb into the wagon. Up to that he had kept silent, which was well enough, seeing I had only to look into his face to know he was proud of me and approving my going; then he took my hand and said:
>
> "Good-bye. Come back a man." (*Autobiography*, p. 115).

That broke him—and Lew wept.

But he cheered up during the long trip: by train to Ohio, by steamboat down the Mississippi, and by Baltimore Clipper to Texas. It would not be an easy road ahead—worst of all would be the inaction—waiting. For some time, the regiment camped on a desolate beach on the Rio Grande delta. All they had to drink was river water, ("a tepid mixture about thirty per cent sand and the rest half yellow mud," *Autobiography* p. 124). Then measles and diarrhea struck—seven died in one day alone. Never would he be able to forget the sound of fife and drum in the nightly dead-march. Soon lumber for coffins was exhausted, then their gun-boxes and cracker barrel staves,—and, finally just blankets as their shrouds. It was a terrible time! And they were anything but alone: elsewhere, thousands of other troops were falling sick as well.

Five long interminable months they waited for action—finally, in December, they were ordered to Monterey. But that wasn't the worst: after tramping 460 miles, they were ordered back to Texas, so Christmas Day of '46, the day they started back was one of utter despair. The regiment was destined to see precious little action. That occurred elsewhere; eventually, in winning the crucial Battle of Buena Vista, Taylor garnished enough glory to win him the U.S. Presidency in '48. To add insult to injury, Taylor falsely accused the Second Indiana Volunteers (Wallace was in the First) of cowardice in battle. For that insult, and for all else he suffered during his year in the war, Wallace never forgave old Zach.

He was mustered out in June of '47, in New Orleans, had all his money ($280) stolen on the steamboat, and arrived back in Indianapolis without any fanfare at all. "In sum, the year had been one of almost unrelieved frustration—inaction, ingloriousness, sordidness, positive humiliation." (McKee, p. 18).

It was a far cry from the dreams he had left with. Here he was, a year later, twenty-years-old, right back where he had started from. And a failed law exam behind him, as well.

One evening, still wondering what he was going to do with his life, whether or not he would marry, he picked up the manuscript of *The Fair God* . . . and did not stop until he had finished reading it, at dawn. Now, it had relevance to him, for he had *been* in Mexico. He resolved to pick up where he had left off.

But Mexico had brought to him long thoughts. Now that he was back home again, they came back to him:

> This evening I picked up a copy of Tupper and read his effusion on "Marriage." This sentence seems familiar to my thoughts, "If thou art to have a wife of thy youth, she is now living on the earth; therefore think of her and pray for weal; yea, though thou hast not seen her."
>
> A thousand times have I had the same idea! Even in childhood we have pleasant vagaries of love. They come to us as views of a clear-blue sky through narrow rifts of dark clouds. We hail them with delight and imagine them heaven. Even in my half-wild boyhood there lived a haunting yearning in my heart to see, hear, and live in presence of her whom Fate was to give me as the wife of my youth.
>
> Many a time have I stood beneath the stars, and gazing up at their bright shinings, mumbled over every form of charm and incantation my fancy conceived, hoping all the time I might accidentally hit upon one which the Chaldees used to subdue by their mysterious power and learn from them the locked-up secrets of the future. Had I been successful the first picture I would have had them paint me would have been the miniature of my unbeheld but somewhere living wife whose name the Destiny of mine had written among "the poetry of Heaven." Not only have I

asked it of the stars, but my curiosity has carried me to more unpoetic lengths. I never meet a good, pretty girl, but I've asked of my soul, expecting its immortality of nature to endow it with at least that much miraculous knowledge, "Is it she?" When will the radiance of that other life fall over mine?

I am a believer in Destiny, and no sceptic to the beautiful theory that the incomplete heart will recognize its perfection instantly it beholds it. I would have made a fiery, energetic follower of Cromwell, or, had I been a Frenchman, would have worshiped the great "N" of *"Le petit Corporal"* with as deep devotion as the Crusader worshiped the holy symbol of his cause. I have always found the enthusiasm of love the wildest, while that of ambition is the steadiest in men's hearts. My noblest dream of life has been one of fame, but my holiest of her whom Fate shall give me for a wife. She must have high qualities to command me. In my aspirations her spirit must follow mine in my war for the world's bubbles, not as a squaw her savage husband, but by my side, a woman's yet an equal spirit. Then I shall tread the *steppes* of a new existence with her. When will my dream come true?

What a place for dreaming was Old Mexico! There in the introspection of idleness my ideals almost took shape.

Many a time have I lain on the soft sand, and while the ocean poured its eternal hymn in my scarce conscious sense, watched the cold, round moon as she looked down on the shadows of night and the seething foam of the waters, and tortured imagination to give me a picture of the beloved, the unbeheld. I have somewhere read a wild legend of a German hunter, who, in some of his wanderings amid the Hartz mountains, came across a romantic cascade. Tired, wearied out, he lay down on its banks and went to sleep. In his slumber a form (a woman's) appeared to his vision. And the form was lovely, transparent as a moonbeam, and bright as a star-halo. It addressed him in terms of love, and seemed to watch over him while he slept. After his slumber passed away he returned home. But the vision of the cascade haunted his memory, and in vain he sought to shake it off. Under its influence he revisited the fountain. Again the wild, beautiful spirit greeted him with its low voice. Then a frantic love assumed the mastery of the hunter's heart. Day after day, night after night, his wasting form was laid on the green bank of the singing waterfall. Ever he sighed, murmured, dreamed. The strength forsook his limbs—the blood melted away in his heart. He loved the water-spirit to madness, but she was of the race of souls and as such could not interwed a mortal. To possess her, therefore, he must die. So, one day when the earth was all bright but his heart all dark, while the fairy sang him a song of unimaginable melody, he stretched his arms to grasp the shadowy enchantress, and plunged over into the roaring caldron of the cascade.

My Egeria is of the race of mortals. I shall go to her for wisdom, as Numa did to his, and to win her I need not die. She is waiting for me somewhere in the cool shadows of tonight, and I wait for her.

She will love me, and I shall make her famous by my pen and glorious by my sword. (*Autobiography*, pp. 197-199).

Vows to a man like Wallace were taken very seriously: they gave him goals to aim at. He was, in his life, to fulfill every word of this vow.

And what did this knight look like? In a letter written by Mary Clemmer is this description:

"Lewis Wallace, of Indiana, is in outward seeming our hero of Provence wearing the bright spurs won on the field of Fornovo. The youthful chevalier *sans peur et sans reproche*, valiant, wise, and loyal.

"He is fashioned of the refined clay of which nature is most sparing, nearly six feet high [actually, he was 5'9"], perfectly straight, with a fine fibred frame all nerve and muscle, and so thin he cannot weigh more than a hundred and thirty pounds. He has profuse black hair, a dark, beautiful face, correct in every line, keen, black eyes deeply set, with a glance that on occasion may cut like fine steel. Black beard and mustache conceal the firm mouth and chin. His modest, quiet manner is the only *amende* that can be made for being so handsome. In a crowd anywhere you would single him out as a king of men.

"Marked for action rather than words, he is habitually reticent, yet when the time comes for speech is ready with eloquent words, given with a voice at once sweet and strong. A man of convictions, earnest in every nerve of his being, intensely earnest." (*Autobiography*, pp. 199-200).

In the city of Crawfordsville lived a wealthy merchant by the name of Major Isaac C. Elston; his house was the finest in the country, as were its furnishings. People came from miles around just to look. Wallace went too, wanting to see for the first time . . . "a sofa" . . . and "a piano." College commencement, in '48 drew him back again. At one of the city homes open for visitors, Wallace wandered in. Over half a century later, he remembered that evening as if it were but yesterday:

> In the midst of the gayety, Major Elston's third daughter appeared. Susan, then eighteen, recently from her graduation at a Quaker school for girls in Poughkeepsie, New York, bearing herself modestly as a veiled nun.

Fifty years and more! I can blow the time aside lightly as smoke from a cigar, and have a return of that evening with Miss Elston, and her blue eyes, wavy hair, fair face, girlish manner, delicate person, and witty flashes to vivify it.

There are young people who think a man past seventy may not be moved by the love of his youth, if he has recollections of it at all. The opinion, I assure them, is an attack upon themselves—they who are in turn to grow old. There was never one, albeit beyond the sage's limit of life, to forget the days he went wooing. Some there are, doubtless, the unsuccessful for instance, who would like to forget them. Be the truth told simply. Far from so much as dimming the recollection, the years but make it holier, until after awhile the old man, nothing loath to expose his whole life else, keeps that dear property to himself. So much I extract from my own experience.

Yet, having undertaken to write my life, would the life be complete without the story of how it became subject to its most benign influence? Let me not falter in confession here. What of success has come to me, all that I am, in fact, is owing to her, the girl of whom I am speaking. The admission is broad, yet it leaves justice but half done.
She was beautiful in my eyes when I first saw her; and the word is not used in its common sense; dolls are pretty; so are faces in wax, if only they are fresh and clean. The beauty she gave me to see that evening in the social blaze was after Wordsworth's ideal:

"A countenance in which did meet
Sweet records, promises as sweet;
A creature not too bright and good
For human nature's daily food,
For transient sorrows, simple wiles,
Praise, blame, love, kisses, tears, and smiles."

The promises were in her face when next I saw her in plain daylight; and after all the trials of years come and gone—now—the same promises are as bank-notes redeemed, and there is no need of them more.

When May 6, 1902 comes round, and repeats itself in budding roses, it will be golden-wedding day with us. The advent may freshen recollection of the glad time, and I bid it welcome in advance, but I will not for that delay the record I have for her as my wife. I have been subject to her; and her gentle soul has controlled me, and bent me to her wishes, but unselfishly, and always for my good, and always so deftly that I was as one blind to the domination. My temper has never been so hot she could not lay it. She has decided me in doubt, defended me against interruptions, saved me my time at the sacrifice of her own, cheered me when down at heart, lured me back to my tasks when the tempter would have whisked me away, held my hand in defeat, and rejoiced with me in my triumphs. In my work she has helped me to the word, and been my one honest critic. Often in the long journey when, at the parting of the ways, I have stopped bewildered, afraid to go on, unwilling to go back, she has set me in the right way, and even gone before to assure me. Her faith in me began with the beginning, when I was unknown and uncertain of myself, and the world all too ready to laugh at my attempts. Hers is a high nature, a composite of genius, commonsense, and all best womanly qualities. The marvel, her memory, has always been at my service. Most fortunately for me, the books she loves are the best, and she knows them by heart. With her in call, I have no use for dictionaries of quotation.

Nor less is she a musician. Not as the divas are, to fill vast interiors and astonish audiences in multitude, but a minnesinger loving to soothe vexed children with lullabies, and set old people to living their lives over again with ballads redolent of things noble and good. Now, grievous to say, a tone has gone out of her voice, and I miss it, and so does she. Sometimes she speaks of it as one of the robberies of old time, but I say no, and insist that she does not practice enough. Still, of long evenings, when the house is quiet and the fire burns, she will bring out the guitar, and with fingers loyal to her feeling as ever, give me the song I have all along most loved, and which, should she be near when I come to die, I would have her sing for the help there will be in it to the spirit crossing the bar. There may be a reader curious to see the lines; and I give them:

"THREE DREAMS

"I dreamed a dream of boyhood's days,
Of high and wild and careless glee.
Around my path ten thousand rays
Sparkling and dancing seemed to be.

"Dream of my boyhood, stay, O stay!
Let me thus sport my life away.
Dream of my boyhood, stay, O stay! --
Alas, alas! It fades away.

"I dreamed a dream of early youth,
A wilderness of sweetest dreams.
I scarce know what of love and truth
Bathing my soul in heavenly beams.

"Dream of my youth, sweet dream, O stay!
Let me thus love my life away.
Dream of my youth, sweet dream, O stay! --
Alas, alas! It fades away!

"I dreamed a dream of Manhood's prime,
Mixed dream of triumph and of strife;

But she at morn and evening's chime
Was there to bless and cheer my life.

"Dream of my prime, stay, O stay!
Thy features court the opening day.
Dream of my prime, stay, O stay! --
Alas, thou too must fade away."
(*Autobiography*, pp. 207-210).

Once having found the *one*, he did not rest until he had won her. And there were many suitors. When finally she accepted his love, it was with the understanding that marriage would have to wait until he could support her:

Three years we waited, and then I led her home, she trusting me when no one else did.

Long, long afterwards she wrote me "A Song of Songs." Here is one verse:

"Our morning dreams are broken,
And castles day by day
With far and floating banners
In distance fade away.
Dim arcade and airy tower
I never more may see,
But all my lost ideals
Are found again in thee."
(*Autobiography*, p. 212)

The fall of '49, Wallace again took the bar examination. Three or four days later, he received "a carefully sealed official envelope addressed, 'Lewis Wallace, Esquire, Attorney-at-Law.' It contained two enclosures: one, the coveted license, signed 'Isaac Blackford, Judge'; the other, a brief explanatory note over the same signature with a postscript—'Permit me to congratulate you upon your safe return from Mexico.'"

Early in 1850, he opened a law office on Covington's muddy main street. Inside, he had a table, a stove, revised Indiana statutes, other law books, and a violin to play when the rest of the town was asleep.

Another attorney, Daniel W. Voorhees, opened up his office about the same time he did. One afternoon some time later Voorhees came into his office and asked a rhetorical question:

"What are you doing?" he asked.

"Nothing."

"Well, it is the same with me; so I propose we chip in and hire a horse and buggy and go to Danville."

The reference was Danville, Illinois.

"What's going on there?"

"Court is in session—that's all."

We reached the town about dusk and stopped at the tavern. The bar-room, when we entered it after supper, was all a-squeeze with residents, spiced with parties to suits pending, witnesses, and jurors. The ceiling was low, and we had time to admire the depth and richness of the universal smoke-stain of the wooden walls. To edge in we had to bide our time. Every little while there would be bursts of laughter, and now and then a yell of delight. At last, within the zone of sight, this was what we saw: In front of us a spacious pioneer fireplace all aglow with a fire scientifically built. On the right of the fireplace sat three of the best storytellers of Indiana, Edward A. Hannegan, Dan Mace, and John Pettit. Opposite them, a broad brick hearth intervening, were two strangers to me whom inquiry presently identified as famous lawyers and yarn-spinners of Illinois.

One may travel now from the Kennebec to Puget Sound and never see such a tournament as the five men were holding; only instead of splintering lances they were swapping anecdotes. As to the kind and color of the jokes submitted to the audience, while not always chaste, they never failed to hit home.

The criss-crossing went on till midnight, and for a long time it might not be said whether Illinois or Indiana was ahead. There was one of the contestants; however, who arrested my attention early, partly by his stories, partly by his appearance. Out of the mist of years he comes to me now exactly as he appeared then. His hair was thick, coarse, and defiant; it stood out in every direction. His features were massive, nose long, eyebrows protrusive, mouth large, cheeks hollow, eyes gray and always responsive to the humor. He smiled all the time, but never once did he laugh outright. His hands were large, his arms slender and disproportionately long. His legs were a wonder, particularly when he was in narration; he kept crossing and uncrossing them; sometimes it actually seemed he was trying to tie them into a bow-knot. His dress was more than plain; no part of it fit him. His shirt collar had come from the home laundry innocent of starch. The black cravat about his neck persisted in an ungovernable affinity with his left ear. Altogether I thought him the gauntest, quaintest, and most positively ugly man who had ever attracted me enough to call for study. Still, when he was in speech, my eyes did not quit his face. He held me in unconsciousness. About midnight his competitors were disposed to give in; either their stores were exhausted, or they were tacitly conceding him the crown. From answering them story for story, he gave two or three to their one. At last he took the floor and held it. And looking back, I am now convinced that he frequently invented his replications; which is saying he possessed a marvelous gift of improvisation. Such was Abraham Lincoln. And to be perfectly candid, had one stood at my elbow that night in the old tavern and whispered: "Look at him closely. He will one day be president and the savior of his country," I had laughed at the idea but a little less heartily than I laughed at the man. Afterwards I came to know him better, and then I did not laugh. (*Autobiography*, pp. 221-223).

Lew and Susan were married on May 6, 1852. That year, he was re-elected Prosecuting Attorney; but two months later, the couple decided to move to Crawfordsville, a larger city with more potential.

By 1853, he had completed the first draft of *The Fair God*; and three years later, he was elected State Senator. But he had not forgotten his vow. Everywhere he looked, he could see signs of trouble. Unless a miracle occurred, sooner or later there would be war between North and South. And when that day came *this time,* he determined, he would be ready. So it was that in 1856, he organized a voluntary company of infantry, The Montgomery Guards. The dress was exotic: that of the famed Zouaves of French Algeria fame. When they would parade, the whole city would turn out to watch. Wallace had concluded that, not being a West Pointer like his father, if war came, the fastest rise to the top would come in the infantry, simply because it involved the bulk of the troops, hence that is where he specialized.

Then it was the summer of '58, and the big giant and the little giant, Abraham Lincoln and Stephen A. Douglas were battling it out for the U.S. Senate in Illinois. At this time, Wallace supporting the Democrats, Douglas was his hero. He determined to hear their next debate.

To me Mr. Douglas was the first of living orators. What a magnificent spectacle he had presented standing day after day alone in the Senate, flinging answers, now to the abolitionists, now to the slave-holders, now to Mr. Seward, now to the arch-conspirator, Jefferson Davis! At such times he was in my eyes a lion bated by foxes and jackals. That Mr. Lincoln—gaunt, awkward, comic Lincoln whom I had seen in the bar-room of the old tavern at Danville—could get the better of him in debate was ludicrous as a mot of the uncouth clown himself. Yet if he could not get the better of my "Little Giant," he could at least draw him fully out upon all the phases of the mighty clash about Slavery and the Extension of Slavery.

In the afternoon of the day of the fourth meeting of the disputants, I found myself in Charleston, Illinois, lost in a crowd assembled in a grove near that interesting little city. The platform for the speakers reminded me of an island barely visible in a restless sea—so great was the gathering. By good management I succeeded in getting standing-room close up in front of the platform.

Mr. Douglas was first to appear. It had not been my good-fortune to have had sight of him before; now I recognized him by his pictures, a short man with a deep chest, Websterian head, and a countenance somewhat lowering. He seemed worried, and took seat with the air of one too closely occupied with thoughts to notice or care for surroundings. It struck me, also, that he was niggardly in his recognition of friends.

Presently there was a commotion in the crowd and a general looking that way, and Mr. Lincoln mounted the steps. He paused on the platform, and took a look over the crowd and into the countenances near by, and there was a smile on his lips and a whole world of kindness in his eyes. The thin neck craned out over his sweat-wilted shirt collar while he bowed to acquaintances. Mr. Douglas's outer suit had come from an accomplished tailor; Mr. Lincoln's spoke of a slop-shop. The multitude impressed me as the most undemonstrative of all I had ever seen on a political occasion. Every man of them, however, was palpitating with an anxiety too great for noise. So, I fancy, men must behave when they are spectators of a duel to the death.

At Ottawa, Mr. Douglas had presented a number of questions to Mr. Lincoln, which that gentleman answered at the Freeport meeting and countered by interrogatories on his side. It resulted that when the two came to Charleston the issues between them were all joined.

When time was called—if I may use the expression—Mr. Lincoln arose, straightening himself as well as he could. But for the benignant eyes, a more unattractive man I had never seen thus the centre of regard by so many people. His voice was clear without being strong. He was easy and perfectly self-possessed. The great audience received him in utter silence, and the July sun beat mercilessly upon his bare head.

Now, not having been blessed with a vision of the events to come, which were to set this uncouth person in a niche high up alongside Washington, leaving it debatable which of the two is greatest, I confess I inwardly laughed at him; only the laugh was quite as much at the political manager who had led him out against Mr. Douglas. Nevertheless, I gave him attention. Ten minutes—I quit laughing. He was getting hold of me. The pleasantry, the sincerity, the confidence, the amazingly original way of putting things, and the simple, unrestrained manner withal, were doing their perfect work; and then and there I dropped an old theory, that to be a speaker one must needs be graceful and handsome. Twenty minutes—I was listening breathlessly, and with a scarcely defined fear. I turned from him to Mr.

Douglas frequently, wondering if the latter could indeed be so superior to this enemy as to answer and overcome him. Thirty minutes—the house divided against itself was looming up more than a figure of speech. My God, could it be prophetic! An hour—the limit of the speech. Mr. Lincoln took his seat. How many souls sat down with him—that is, how many of the unbelieving like myself were converted to his thinking—I could not know; yet of one thing I was assured—it was in somebody's intention to do the old government to death, and slavery was to be the excuse for the crime. Nor could I get from under a conviction that Mr. Lincoln's speech was a defence of Freedom.

Then Mr. Douglas arose. As his stumpy figure appeared, provoking comparison with his tall rival, I was amused thinking, what if in an alignment of company they should be required to dress right or left upon each other? He had an hour and a half for reply. Despite my predilections, I was driven shortly to acknowledge that the prepossession did not belong to him. His face was darkened by a deepening scowl, and he was angry; and in a situation like this anger is always an admission in the other party's favor. He spoke too gutturally, also, that it was difficult to understand him. Still he was my Gamaliel. From him I had my politics. He failed to draw me like his competitor; he had no magnetism; he was a mind all logic; at the same time, be it said in truth, Stephen A. Douglas could not make a poor speech. I listened almost prayerfully. Whereas Mr. Lincoln had been the fine flower of courtesy, Mr. Douglas made no return in kind. What could be the matter? Afterwards I knew. He was handicapped by a continuous terror lest he should say something that would lose him the support of the South in the vastly more important convention then shortly to be held at Charleston, South Carolina. I did not stay to hear him through, but left carrying with me a damaging contrast—while Mr. Lincoln had been the advocate of Freedom, Mr. Douglas, with all his genius for discussion, had not been able to smother the fact that he was indirectly and speciously acknowledging all the South claimed for slavery.

So Lincoln came into my view a second time. (*Autobiography*, pp. 252-256).

The winter of '60, Wallace was invited to a Democratic caucus in Indianapolis. Once there, he discovered that it was for the purpose of secession. Appalled, he walked out, then, almost immediately, walked over toward the Capitol, and knocked on the door of Governor Morton's office. Morton had switched parties two years previously, and Wallace hadn't spoken to him since.

> The governor, when I went into his office, was sitting at the farther end under a window writing. He came forward at sight of me, and took my hand cordially. Doubtless he remembered, as did I, that we had been school-boys together. Declining his invitation to sit, I began at once.
>
> "Governor, I owe you an apology for what I have been saying of you politically. You were right in quitting the Democratic party. Now I, too, will quit it."
>
> He called me familiarly: "Well, Lew, this does not astonish me. Never mind what you have been saying about me. Tell me what has happened—something serious, I know."
>
> "Yes, I now know that war is certain, and soon, and that the South will make it."
>
> "How do you know it?"
>
> Carefully withholding the names of any of the men I had seen at the meeting in room fourteen, I told the governor

then what had taken place and been said; after which I concluded, saying: "If these leaders are right, governor, and the South does attempt forcible secession, I tender you my services in advance. You may command me absolutely."

He took my hand again, his eyes humid.

"You could not go with the South," he said, "or with any treasonable organization here at home. That is not in your blood. I tell you, also in advance, if the South goes to the extreme of war, or threatens it by any overt act, I will send for you first man."

Thereupon I thanked him, and took my leave.

Somewhat late in the afternoon of April 13th I was addressing a jury in the Clinton County Circuit Court when the telegraph operator of the town came into the courtroom, and told the judge he had a telegram for me. The judge spoke to me, and the sheriff put into my hand a message in words very nearly these:

"Sumpter has been fired on. Come immediately.
"Oliver P. Morton."

I gave the telegram to the judge to read, and, with his permission, excused myself to the jury, leaving the case to my law partner. (*Autobiography*, pp. 260-261).

By 7 A.M. Sunday morning, Wallace was knocking on the door of the Governor's residence, only to discover he was already at his office. Arrived there, the Governor wasted no time: Lincoln had called for 75,000 volunteers and he wanted Indiana to be ready with its quota (six regiments) first—and he wanted Wallace to take over immediately as Adjutant General. Wallace agreed, on condition that one of the regiments be his. Then he swung into action, gathering together his team, firing communiques all across the state in the Governor's name—and men began to pour in. Each train that came in brought more, and each contingent would be escorted by a brass band, flags, and fife and drum corps, to the State-house. Along the way, cheering thousands lined the sidewalks. At the State-house would be the Governor to welcome and inspire them. From there the men proceeded to temporary quarters; they would have to be fed, housed, and kept busy. It was an administrative nightmare—but the lessons Wallace learned, and the administrative skills honed, would be used again in Cincinnati.

At midnight Friday night, Wallace reported in to the Governor that there were now 130 companies in camp (70 more than the 60 in the Presidential quota!). Wallace chose the Eleventh Regiment as his own. Later that day, the citizens of Indianapolis were treated to the first dress parade by a full regiment ever held in the state.

In perfect symmetry, the Eleventh marched up to the State House, muskets gleaming in the sun. Col. Lew Wallace "sat easily his splendid mount, a blooded roan stallion; he was lithe and darkly handsome, keen and serious as a scimitar, and brightly embellished with gold epaulets, crimson sash, Derringer pistols, and flashing sword. The crowd was immense. The Hon. William E. McLean of Terre Haute eloquently presented the national standard; Miss Abigail Cady of Indianapolis, with an elegantly written address, bestowed the regimental banner which she had richly embroidered. Tears fell freely, amidst rousing "Tigers!" Wallace replied with impressive thanks and promises. He and his regiment, kneeling knightlike, swore to "Remember Buena Vista!" They adopted this cry as their motto; it was directed at Zachary Taylor's libel of 1847, and everybody knew that the leader of the traitors, Jefferson Davis, was Taylor's son-in-law." (McKee, p. 36).

Wallace's rise to the top would be meteoric.

By June, he and his 500 Zouaves marched double-time (a standard attack characteristic of Zouave troops) all night on a surprise attack in Romney, Virginia. The 1200 rebel troops there fled as they heard them coming. The press pounced upon the story: the newspapers, *Leslie's Illustrated Weekly* and *Harper's Weekly* made much of it. In two months of war, prior to this, little had happened. There was all the action anyone would have ever wanted after that—but then it was back to Indianapolis, for they had only enlisted for *three months!* Most everyone had felt the war would be over by that time.

This time it took a month to get another regiment together, for the term was now three *years!* By October, Wallace was promoted to Brigadier General. But he chafed because of inaction. Then, he got together with Grant in the bold attacks on Forts Herman, Henry, and Donelson on the Tennessee and Cumberland Rivers. The first two forts fell; and by February 14, their 25,000 men were closing in on Fort Donelson and its 15,000 defenders; Wallace's forces held the center of an attacking horseshoe. It was a bitterly cold night, and Wallace was up early. Astride his magnificent horse "John," he made an unforgettable picture which Col. John Thayer, a brigade commander, never forgot. "The sun was barely rising of a cold, frosty morning. General Wallace was a princely figure, particularly in the saddle, and he rode ... a single-stepper that was the pride of the division. As he came up, his military accoutrements flashing in the red light of the rising sun, and the charger moving as though to the sound of music, he presented a sight that is not seen more than once in a lifetime." (McKee, pp. 42-3).

Then battle raged; during one attack, he ordered 5,000 troops to charge up a three-hundred-yard slope to the Confederate advance trenches. By 5 P.M., they were at the top. Wallace was first into the fort, to accept its surrender. The victory brought with it, according to Grant, "the greatest number of prisoners of war ever taken in one battle on this continent." (McKee, p. 45).

Leslie's made much of the victory and gave more credit to Wallace than he deserved. Wallace kept a close eye on the press and the historical records being tabulated, and made sure he was given credit where credit was due. Late in March, Wallace was raised in rank to Major General, the highest rank legally attainable—and he was the youngest man to have it.

He did not know it—but he was on the peak.

Jealousy lifted its ugly head. After Donelson, the whole South lay open before Grant and his associate generals. But one man had seniority, grim-faced General Henry W. Halleck—and neither of them liked each other very much. Halleck was a brilliant theorist but only mediocre when he tried to put his theories into practice. After the great victory, in fact, Halleck spitefully removed Grant from command, and, even worse, had him in house arrest. Grant's command was restored, but at a great cost in morale and momentum. And General Don Carlos Buell, with his huge army, was a maverick and refused to be led by anyone else. As a result of all this infighting, Union forces lost a priceless opportunity to end the war. By the time they were finally ready to move again, the enemy had regrouped and rebuilt.

Wallace and fellow general, Charles Smith, could quite possibly have changed the course of the war had not Smith taken a terrible fall leaving Wallace's campground. In so much agony was he that Wallace urged him to remain for treatment. He did not—and died of complications not long after—so the follow-up attack of the two generals never took place. Thus was opened the door to that great bloodbath, Shiloh.

No small thanks to the in-fighting at the top, the Union high command remained so fragmented, no one person was in control. No one knew what was happening. No one knew where the Confederate troops were, nor how many were where. Leisurely, Grant moved toward Pittsburg landing, nine miles from Savannah. His 35,000 men would soon be joined by Buell's 37,500, and no one could then stand before them.

Unfortunately, he and his associates had no idea that General Joseph Johnston, that brilliant tactician, had 40,000 troops at their very door. In fact, when, on the morning of April 6, Johnston struck, the Pearl Harbor of the Civil War took place—Shiloh. *No one* was ready, and just as sentries ran into camps telling of the attack, the Rebels were upon them, catching who knows how many still asleep or just waking, hardly any armed. It was a massacre! Blissfully unaware, Grant was in Savannah, so there was no one to respond quickly.

The land ran crimson with blood, and as the sun rose and declined, it degenerated into wholesale butchery on both sides. All day long, the shooting, stabbing, hacking, and clubbing continued. Before the sun set, 15,000 men were dead, wounded, or missing. The Union Army of the Tennessee was reeling at the edge of the river—it looked like it was all over. General Johnston, seeing that no one would lead a charge, decided to lead it himself. But . . . , one of the Union soldiers fleeing ahead of the charge, turned and randomly shot behind him—mortally wounding the great general. Had that terrible loss to the South not occurred, had Beauregard charged once more, our history might read much differently. As it was—the line held.

Meanwhile, Wallace was awaiting orders from Grant: he knew by the heavy firing that a great battle was going on but could do nothing about it. Uninformed of the Army's retreat, he marched his 6,500 men miles in the wrong direction, thus not catching up with the other forces until after dark. Also, after dark, came Buell.

It rained heavily during the night, but, in spite of it, Grant was ready by dawn and, with his reinforcements doubling his army he mercilessly shelled the enemy. It was another terrible day of battle. By 4 P.M., the lop-sided numbers and the absence of Johnston turned the tide, and Confederate forces were on the run. For the two day carnage, the Confederates left 11,000 dead, wounded, or missing; and the Union, 13,000.

Initially, all that Americans heard was that they had won a great victory—and that Grant was the hero. Then, the full story came out. Certain leaders of the press turned vengefully on Grant. Was he drunk that he wasn't *there?* Halleck seized the opportunity to humiliate him, again removing him from command. The same turn of events occurred with Wallace: initially, he was depicted as a hero, then he discovered that he too was being blamed for not being at the right place at the right time. Also, in an ill-advised moment, he opened his big mouth and told some visitors what he thought of Halleck. Half way through, he tried to stop, but in vain: "—I had become a loaded car with broken brakes, rushing on a down-grade." (*Autobiography*, p. 579). After they left, he discovered they were Halleck's aides.

Halleck never forgave him. And since there was blame to be shared by many, not just Grant, after Shiloh, he got attacked as well. But it went further than that: in his obsession to be king of the hill, he had taken verbal potshots at some of his colleagues, and pouted when someone else got more glory than he. In field reports, he even put down Grant while lauding himself. Grant was far more forgiving than Halleck, but it took a long time for him to forget Wallace's failure to give credit where it was due.

Next thing Wallace knew, he had no command—and he was back home in Indiana—on the shelf. He would brood about Shiloh the rest of his life.

He wrote a long letter to General Sherman, pleading his case. Sherman responded with one almost as long, praising him, but telling him to cool down and stop stirring the High Command's kettle. Halleck by now was General-in-Chief, so Wallace had thoroughly boxed himself in.

Lincoln sighed, "A major general once out, it is next to impossible for even the President to get him in again," to Wallace when Wallace pled his case in person. So back to Indiana he went . . . but only for weeks, for he was summoned by Governor Morton to keep General Kirby-Smith and his 16,000 men from taking Frankfort, Kentucky. Seeing a chance to redeem himself, Wallace took command of nine regiments and was well on his way to success when suddenly the overbearing General William Nelson showed up with an order superseding him. Furthermore, he went out of his way to tell Wallace he didn't even want him around. Six days later, Nelson was routed by Kirby-Smith, losing 5,000 men in the process. So Wallace went back to his shelf.

General Horatio G. Wright took him off it and asked him to take command of Cincinnati (then largest city west of Baltimore and north of New Orleans), and save it from the advancing General Heth with his 9,000 men. Here it was that Wallace choreographed the greatest production of his lifetime, for if he was to save "The Queen City of the West," it would have to be mainly with civilians. He had the mayor declare martial law, and as commanding general, ordered 15,000 citizens out with ploughs, picks, shovels, scrapers to construct breastworks ten miles long to protect Cincinnati, Covington, and Newport. In thirty hours, thanks to three city engineers, he had constructed a pontoon bridge across the river (over coal barges!). People streamed in by the thousands from everywhere—and everyone was given something to do; everyone was housed and fed. By the fifth day, he had 72,000 men at work. 55,000 were posted behind the breastworks, 15,000 on the banks of the Ohio. 16 steamboats patrolled the river. And a personal staff of 250 reported to him each day. By the time Kirby-Smith got there, he was too late. The city was saved. Years afterward, Wallace learned that had he taken the city, he would have drained the region dry and demanded at least $15,000,000 ransom. The impact on the war would have been seismic. For the rest of his life, Wallace would be known as "The Savior of Cincinnati."

On the shelf again—but not for long. His old nemesis, General Halleck asked him to take over Camp Chase, near Columbus, there to organize paroled and exchanged prisoners of war and get them ready to fight Indians in Minnesota. Wallace felt Halleck was trying to humiliate him enough so he'd resign, but he decided he'd tough it out. He went out to Columbus, turned it around from the hell-hole it had been when he came—and then most of the now well-clothed men left for home. Then back to the shelf.

Off the shelf next to serve as President of a tribunal investigating the military performance of General Buell. There were daily sessions over a six-month period, in Cincinnati, Louisville, and Nashville. Mr. Ben Pittman, father of American stenography, kept the records. At the end, the results were indeterminant, with some blame, some praise. Then back home to the shelf.

Again, he made himself a nuisance in Washington. Lincoln was willing to give him another chance, Halleck was not. But this time, he was taken off the shelf by Governor Morton. Morgan, the Confederate raider, had crossed the Ohio into Indiana with somewhere between 4,000 and 8,000 men. Wallace arrived, finding the capital in a near panic. He organized 1,300 men, but never had to fight, for Morgan was caught just before crossing the Pennsylvania border. Then back to the shelf.

Finally, Lincoln, over Halleck's protests, decided to step in: he sent for Wallace. In the White House, Lincoln offered him the command of the Middle Department (Delaware and most of Maryland), headquartering in Baltimore (America's third largest city). Lincoln told him that a big election was coming, to handle it wisely; then sent him in to see blunt, curt, icy Secretary of War Stanton. Stanton told him that slavery *must* be abolished in Maryland, and Lincoln endorsed for a second term—all, without overtly using force! And he had only two weeks to pull it off. Feverishly, Wallace went to work. Providentially, he discovered that Maryland still had a governor. Not much of one, for with martial law, Wallace ruled supreme. Wallace took his staff by train to Annapolis, all dressed in their dress attire, and made a call on the flabbergasted and heretofore ignored General Bradford. As a result, the Governor agreed to respond to letters for protection Wallace had received, and ask Wallace to send troops to the polls in those areas. Wallace did so, and the Confederate sympathizers, seeing the troops in areas where they planned to take over the process, withdrew in frustrated rage. Slavery was abolished in Maryland, and Maryland helped keep Lincoln in power.

Shortly afterwards, Wallace received by courier a small visiting card. It contained a request.

Will Gen. Wallace call
and see me?

                    A. Lincoln.

When Wallace got to the White House, the President received him cordially. "I sent for you," he said, "to say that I watched the boiling of the kettle over in Maryland, and I think you managed it beautifully. It was a good thing, that getting Governor Bradford between you and the enemy here in Congress." Then Lincoln sent him, with a personal letter, to Stanton. Unbelievably, to Wallace, Stanton shook his hand warmly, commending him with one of his rare "Well dones."

Gradually, Wallace consolidated his position in Baltimore, making friends with all the thought-leaders in his district. One of them, who he grew to respect very much, was one of the most powerful men in America: John W. Garrett, President of the Baltimore & Ohio Railroad. About July 2 of '64, Garrett came to call on him, obviously concerned about something. By the time he was through, Wallace too was apprehensive: railroad employees were reporting more and more sightings of Confederate troops in the Shenandoah Valley. If this continued, and they united in force, what would stand in their way to keep them from taking Washington? Before leaving, Garrett called Wallace's attention to the iron bridge at Monocacy Junction. Would Wallace protect it if it was attacked? Wallace promised, little dreaming that it would ever happen.

So, Wallace began taking stock; he discovered that while there were 53 forts and 22 batteries defending the city, it took 37,000 men to man them—and there were currently only about half that many. Worse yet, most of those were convalescents or invalids. General Sigel at Richmond could not field more than 6,000 men if he were attacked. As for General Hunter, the commander to the north, he was supposedly fighting somewhere near Lynchburg.

Wallace shuddered: all the gateways out of the Shenandoah Valley were wide open. If Lee were to notice—nothing could save

Washington. Halleck had agreed to notify Grant immediately if there were any significant troop concentrations near Washington so troops could be rushed there quickly. The next day, Wallace became even more alarmed. He called his Adjutant General, Col. Lawrence, and asked how many troops they could pull in from the large area they controlled: the entire Chesapeake region. The total was terribly small: only about 2,300 effective.

Only hours later, Lawrence brought him a telegram in haste: It was from General Sigel and read: "I have reports of an advance of the enemy in force down the Shenandoah Valley. His advance is at Winchester." Wallace immediately sent out orders to his chief officers to get ready for action. General Tyler, he ordered to Monocacy Junction with his entire command.

On July 4, he telegraphed Halleck of what he had done . . . also the report he had just received. Martinsburg has been evacuated, Sigel falling back to Harper's Ferry. Estimates of the enemy: 10,000 to 20,000, infantry and artillery.

Then a telegram from Tyler at Monocacy: All telegraph communication cut west of Frederick. Now thoroughly alarmed, Wallace decided to leave Baltimore and join Tyler at the Monocacy Bridge, asking Garrett to have a locomotive ready for him by midnight, and clear the track to the bridge. He did not tell Halleck, knowing that if he were wrong in his surmises, it could cost him his command. At midnight, with only Col. Ross accompanying him, he climbed into the locomotive cab, and gave the signal.

Behind the scenes, the federal attack had indeed been planned by Lee, sending General Early on this surprise attack, with 17,000 men, up the Shenandoah Valley. Within a week he had taken control of everything clear to the Potomac, had destroyed a section of the B&O Railroad, and had ignited part of Hagerstown.

For good measure, the two generals assigned to protect the region, Hunter and Sigel, were in flight. Civilian refugees thronged the roads leading north and east. But Grant told Halleck not to worry: Early is not anywhere near the Potomac! Halleck, in a stormy interview with Stanton, backed Grant's statement. Not until the fifth, when the Confederate Army was actually crossing the Potomac did Grant realize his error and offer to send more troops. A disaster much worse than Shiloh loomed ahead!

Only Wallace, with 2,300 men, stood between Early's 17,000 men and disaster for the Republic. He sent out scouts in all directions, and urged Halleck to send reinforcements; instead, Halleck sent them to Harper's Ferry where they *weren't* needed! And most of the 2,300 men he *did* have were untried in battle. He felt alone—yet, he also realized that perhaps this would be his finest hour, the opportunity to redeem himself after Shiloh. As more and more reports came in, confirming the size of the approaching army, he knew he could never hold them—he could only delay them long enough for Grant to send in reinforcements. Every *minute* he held them back was one minute more in the greater battle to save the nation. For if Early would extort over $200,000 out of little Frederick, imagine the price of Washington! Wallace shuddered at what he was standing in the way of. If Early took Washington, the naval yards and all the ships would either be destroyed or taken—same for Baltimore, only 30 miles away. In the Treasury were untold millions of bonds, and other millions ready to be issued. There were storehouses filled with property of all kinds: medical, military weapons and ammunition, commissary, the accumulation of years. And the city itself with all its beautiful buildings: the Capitol, the White House, the Library of Congress—and worst nightmares of all, President Lincoln, cloaked and hooded, in flight. (*Autobiography*, p. 726).

Lee and the South, with Washington and Baltimore as hostage, would have been in the driver's seat: the North would have been at their mercy.

All this went through Wallace's mind as events unfolded around him. Col. Clendenin with 250 cavalry rode in; then Brigadier General Ricketts en route west was stopped by Wallace, and he agreed to stay, bringing Wallace's total forces to around 6,000 men, barely a third of Early's. For a while, his cavalry held Frederick, then had to gradually give way.

Around 7 A.M. the morning of July 9, the real Battle of Monocacy began. As the firing began, Wallace remembered snatches of "Horatius at the Bridge." About 10:30 A.M., under cover of tremendous artillery fire, the Confederates attempted to storm the Union forces. For five and a half hours, Wallace's troops threw back wave after wave. By that time, 1,500 men were dead or wounded. And Wallace's only big gun, a twenty-four pounder—was wrecked by a recruit who rammed the shell in before the cartridge.

After the war, Wallace would discover that Early never dreamed there was a force this large between him and Washington; had he known, he would have crossed the Potomac at Edwards Ferry just below Harper's Ferry—and no power on earth could have saved Washington.

Finally, Wallace knew that to fight any longer would be to doom the rest of his men, so he sneaked down to the wooden bridge and fired it. "A great smoke began to fill the sky and blot out the sun. Soon the floor timber fell into the water." (*Autobiography*, p. 778).

At 3 P.M., he again telegraphed Halleck, letting him know his forces had been fighting Early for eight hours; and now Early's reserve forces were massing for an all-out attack—and urging him to strengthen Washington's defenses. At last, around 4 P.M., after having given Washington one more day, for it was too late for Early to move much that day, Wallace signaled retreat towards Baltimore.

When Early's forces came in view of the Capitol on July 12, he saw through his field glasses long lines of reinforcements filing into Fort Stevens. *He was one day too late!*

For a time, the wildest rumors circulated . . . but there was little said in defense of Wallace, for his having delayed Early just long enough. Stanton ridiculed him, Halleck sneered, even Lincoln gave Wallace no praise in his telegram to Grant. For three days, Wallace was removed, by order of Grant—and panic reigned in Baltimore. (McKee, p. 73).

But then reports began to come in, and a truer picture of events began to take shape. Even Stanton reversed himself, telling Wallace that the battle had been "timely, well-delivered, well-managed, and saved Washington City." The *Baltimore American* lauded him, Horace Greeley noted that Wallace could have honorably signaled his retreat long before he did. Grant conceded that he had delayed Early long enough to save Washington. One of the plaques in the Monocacy Battlefield reads:

"These men died to save the National

Capitol, and they *did* save it."

Two months later, Grant invited him to come over to City Point for a visit. Grant was most genial, and introduced him to everybody, and acted as if nothing negative had ever occurred between them.

Early's "almost" capture of Washington represented the last major Confederate offensive, so there was no opportunity for Wallace to get back into battle action. But Baltimore was now so calm that he searched for excitement elsewhere. Chatting with Lincoln one day, the subject of Maximilian and Carlotta and the

French Empire in Mexico came up. Both worried about the back door. What was there to prevent Confederate leaders from retreating into Mexico? What could the U.S. do about it? Wallace suggested that Lincoln aid General Juarez, help drive out the French, and help slam the door on Confederate influence on Mexican affairs. Lincoln referred him to Grant, and Grant granted him leave from Baltimore so he could go down to Texas, and then see what might be done. But Lincoln urged caution and secrecy: he didn't want to rile Napoleon right then if he could avoid it.

Intertwined with his desire to get rid of the French and block the Confederates was the long harbored yearning to find El Dorado. Perhaps, somewhere, somehow, in the process of serving his country, he could gain an interest in Mexico's silver mines. Off and on over the next four or five years, he would shuttle back and forth to Mexico, hoping that he would be given the opportunity to lead an invasion. Along the way, he entered into a great deal of Keystone Cops intrigue—he was too trusting to be very good at cloak and dagger things. Along the way, he became acquainted with Benito Juarez, Mexico's George Washington, and was instrumental in helping to arm 7,000 of Juarez's soldiers. Eventually, the French left, Maximilian was executed in June of '64, and Juarez took over all Mexico. Meanwhile, each trip Wallace took to Mexico deepened his love for it. For all these years of effort, and expending thousands of dollars of his own money, Mexico eventually reimbursed him $15,000 in 1882.

Then came the assassination of Lincoln—and the Union was plunged into mourning. The nation was not only in shock, but there was great fear everywhere. Was this just an isolated incident, or was it a broadly-based conspiracy? Were other key government leaders to be next? Sadly, the new President, Andrew Johnson, had no mandate, no following, no constituency, and was prisoner of forces beyond his control. In this state of paranoia, a military tribunal was set up to try those accused of being accomplices.

Wallace had been in charge of Lincoln's body as it lay in state in Baltimore, where thousands passed by to pay their last respects. Now he was asked to be part of the most dramatic and far-reaching trial in American history. Never before had a President been assassinated. The war itself was by far the bloodiest in our history. In the South, one-in-four men were either dead or incapacitated for life: it was widely rumored that Jefferson Davis himself was involved in the conspiracy.

On the bench were eight celebrated Union generals (David Hunter, Lew Wallace, August Kautz, Albion Howe, Robert Foster, James Ekins, T. M. Harris, and Joseph Holt) and two colonels (Charles Tomkins and David Clendenin). The eight accused were George A. Atzerodt, Lewis Payne, Edwin Spangler, Michael O'Laughlin, Samuel Arnold, David Heroth, Dr. Samuel A. Mudd, and Mary E. Surratt. These were accused of conspiring to kill Lincoln, Johnson, Seward, Grant, etc. The stage for this drama was a large room in Washington's old Penitentiary Building.

It was a long trial, during that hot summer of '65, involving 336 witnesses! Wallace was chosen as the second ranking member because of his legal background. It was not easy for the judges because their military superiors, from the President on down, made it abundantly clear that they wanted punishment. The people demanded victims for the war and the President's death; therefore such niceties as civil liberties were not to get very much in the way. In war-time, martial law takes precedence over civil law—and this was a war-time tribunal of military officers. Both Wallace and Holt felt that Rebels had *no rights*, and they considered the eight to be Rebels. During the entire trial, the eight accused were hooded and shackled so they couldn't communicate with each other.

Thus it should come as no surprise that the prosecution objections were sustained almost all the time and defense almost not at all. Civil libertarians were appalled that Wallace, at least, didn't serve as a counter force, and speak up for the rights of the accused. At the end, all eight were convicted. But, under ordinary circumstances, no court would have convicted Mrs. Surratt (John Wilkes Booth's landlady), Dr. Mudd (the physician who attended Booth's wounds), Edwin Spangler (a scene-shifter), O'Laughlin, or Arnold. The court condemned to death Herold, Atzerodt, Payne (bloody assaulter of Seward and his household), and Mary Surratt. Later on, Holt was discredited for suppressing evidence which proved Surratt's innocence. These four were hanged two days after the trial.

For two years, those in the Tribunal were considered heroes; later, however, the full story came out, and the principals were stained. Eventually, Stanton (who pulled the strings behind the scenes) was discharged from his office, and the President pardoned Spangler, Arnold, and Mudd. Poor O'Laughlin died of smallpox contracted in the Dry Tortuga prison.

Next, Wallace was asked to serve as President of a Tribunal trying Henry Wirz, commander of the infamous Andersonville Prison in Georgia (and afterward, it was hoped, Jefferson Davis). For two months, a parade of over 300 witnesses testified, and, as before, civil liberties were disregarded. The attitude, from Stanton on down was that, in war—and afterwards --, a soldier does not spare an enemy. From 1863 till the end of the war, this 26½ acre military prison (actually, an open stockade) held a total of 49,485 prisoners, of which 13,737 died there! Suffering from congestion, insufficient food, exposure, pollution of water, and disease—was so terrible "Andersonville" has become known as the ultimate Civil War hell-hole. The Tribunal found it very difficult to find anyone who would come forward as a defense witness, for the North was outraged.

It would not be until long after that the public learned that Grant had refused to exchange prisoners; had he done so, who knows how many thousands of these men would have lived! And Wirz, he was but one of the overseers who took commands from higher up. But, here too, the Government and the people demanded a scapegoat: Wirz was hanged.

Actually, things were rather even. During the war, Union Troops had captured 222,000 prisoners, the Confederates 210,000. 26,000 Southerners died in Northern camps while only 22,000 Northerners died in Southern camps—but most of *those* were in Andersonville.

Back in Crawfordsville, Wallace continued to write, puttered around at the bank and in his law practice. But what he really wanted was an appointment, preferably a consulship—America didn't have ambassadors yet—in places like Bolivia or Brazil. But Grant didn't offer anything he and his wife wanted.

In Crawfordsville, the three daughters and two sons of Col. Elston all lived in homes in the 40-50 acre Elston tract; each morning, the five married daughters called on Mrs. Elston the matriarch. Wallace was already participating in Civil War veteran gatherings or as presiding officer or luminary at gatherings everywhere.

With the year 1872, *The Fair God* was at last done. That fall, he took the train east and waited upon James R. Osgood of Boston. Osgood and his editorial team liked what they saw, so by summer of '73, Wallace was back in Boston reading proofs. In August, *The Fair God: Or The Last of the 'Tzins: A Tale of the Conquest of Mexico*, all 175,000 words, was finally published.

The book has great battle scenes—and here Wallace drew heavily from his own real-life war experiences: McKee describes the mix as "a complex of strange, almost unpronounceable names, exotic splendors, dazzling costumes . . . . Likewise the broad sweep of the plot, with its clash between two complex civilizations and its whirlpool of intrigue, heroism, love, piety, superstition, and savagery." (McKee, p. 123).

Reviews were generally positive. John Hay, man of letters and statesman, declared it to be one of the finest novels of the time. The book sold well also: by 1941, 217,000 copies having been sold (7,000 copies sold the first year, but in the next decade it went through 16 more printings; *Ben-Hur*, of course, helped sell even more).

TIRZAH

THREE

Ben-Hur

Then came the bitter Hayes-Tilden campaign of 1876. It was also one of the closest elections in history, with most newspapers conceding that Tilden (184 electoral votes) had beaten Hayes (173); with Louisiana and Florida still too close to call. Grant sent teams of VIPs to those states to "witness" the counting. Wallace was one of them. Result: both states delivered to Hayes, who then became President with fewer popular votes than Tilden. Clearly, the whole thing smelled. On the other hand, so did Tilden's side. About the best that can be said about the whole mess is that neither side had an ethical edge over the other.

Wallace had campaigned extensively for Hayes, so he finally had his reward. This time he *was* offered the position of Minister to Bolivia (at $5,000 a year). Wallace demurred. So another offer came, the Governorship of the New Mexico Territory, a vast area three times the size of Virginia, stretching from California to Texas (and including today's New Mexico, Arizona, and parts of Nevada, Utah, and Colorado), at $2,600 a year; he took New Mexico. Again, fate was on his side.

The Territory was then wide-open country—far more so than Wallace had first realized. And it was wild and lonely, only 6,000 people (mostly Indians and Mexicans) lived in the ancient capital, Santa Fe. It was primitive, dirty, and uncivilized. In short, it was a tough place to bring your family to.

He soon learned about Lincoln County (an area larger than the entire state of Indiana), a powder keg which had exploded into one of the West's most infamous conflicts, the Lincoln County War. It was at its height in 1878 when Wallace arrived. And Billy the Kid was its centerpiece.

Early in 1879, the Governor decided he would have to risk being bushwacked on the 200 mile trek down to Lincoln.

A meeting between the Governor and the famed outlaw took place on March 6, 1879 at the home of John B. Wilson.

> At 9 P.M., the time designated, Wallace heard a knock and called out, "Come in." The door swung slowly open, and there stood the Kid, a Winchester in his right hand and a revolver in his left. He was a mere boy in years and appearance—nineteen, five feet seven, thin, light-haired, blue-eyed. This was the terrible Kid, companion of thieves and murderers since he had quit school at the age of eleven, ruthless killer of at least six men (some said nineteen).
>
> "I was sent for," said the Kid pleasantly, "to meet the governor at nine o'clock. Is he here?"
>
> "I am Governor Wallace."
>
> "Your note gave promise of absolute protection."
>
> "Yes, and I have been true to my promise." Wallace pointed to Wilson and added: "This man, whom of course you know, and I are the only persons in the house."
>
> The Kid lowered his rifle, returned his revolver to its holster and sat down. Wallace unfolded a plan that would let him testify with safety at the trial of Dolan. In order to preserve the Kid from the stigma of informer, his arrest would be arranged as if it were against his will. He would have a strong military guard at all times, especially during the trial, which was to be held in two or three weeks. Wallace closed with the solemn assurance: "In return for your

doing this, I will let you go scot free with a pardon in your pocket for all your misdeeds."
(McKee, p. 150).

Later on,

> "Wallace called upon the Kid and drew from him the names and misdeeds of numerous badmen. The Kid accused Dudley of having turned Fort Stanton into a hideout for Murphy killers. The governor told the Kid of stories current about his marksmanship and, trustingly enough, asked for an exhibition. After he had shown me what he could do, Wallace afterward recalled to a newspaperman, "I complimented him and coupled with my praise the question, 'Billy, isn't there some trick in your shooting? How do you do it?'
>
> "'Well, General,' he replied, 'there is a trick to it. When I lift my revolver, I say to myself, "Point with your finger," and unconsciously it makes the aim certain. There is no failure. I pull the trigger and the bullet goes true to its mark. That's the truck, I suppose, to my shooting.'"
> (McKee, pp. 151-152).

Ignoring threats against his life, Wallace moved ahead in attempting to clean up the Territory. The grand jury returned about 200 indictments. After pleading not guilty to old indictments against him, the Kid got the jitters and rode away to freedom. Then he, too, sent out word that he was gunning for the Governor.

It was not enough that Lincoln County was aflame, the Apaches, under Chief Victorio, were also on the rampage. Victorio's death by a sharpshooter did not help much, because he was followed by Geronimo and Nachez.

In September 1880, Wallace took a two-month leave of absence in order to campaign in Indiana for Garfield. Meanwhile, Billy added some more murders to his account, and Sheriff Pat Garrett captured the outlaw at Stinking Spring, and locked him up in the Santa Fe jail.

> .... the Kid bethought himself of Wallace's promise of clemency, completely overlooking the subsequent murders and thefts which invalidated it. March 4, 1881, he penned a letter to the governor containing a wonderful mixture of blackmail, querulousness, and bravado:
>
> *I expect you have forgotten what you promised me, this month two years ago, but I have not, and I think you had ought to have come and see me.... I have done everything that I promised you I would, and you have done nothing that you promised.... I think when you think the matter over, you will come down, and I can then explain everything to you.... I am not treated right by [U.S. Marshal John] Sherman. He lets every stranger that comes to see me through Curiosity in to see me, but will not let a single one of my friends in, not even an Attorney. I guess they mean to send me up without giving me any show, but they will have a nice time doing it. I am not entirely without friends.*

By way of reply Wallace merely gave the newspaper copies of the correspondence between himself and the Kid. "I presume," Wallace later said, "he understood that the door of my clemency was shut." In April the Kid was convicted of murder, at Mesilla, Doña Ana County, and sentenced to be hanged. Apparently he refused to believe that the door was irrevocably shut, for he told reporters who called at the Lincoln jail: "Considering the active part Governor Wallace took on our side and the friendly relations that existed between him and me, and the promise he made me, I think he ought to pardon me." On April 30 Wallace signed the death warrant.

The paper was already useless. On the evening of April 28 the Kid had snatched a pistol from one of his guards, shot them both, and ridden away. For twelve weeks he roamed about his accustomed haunts, alternately strutting and hiding, unable to tear himself away to the safety of distant but unfamiliar regions, though every other man's hand here was raised against him. At twenty-one, the paragon of badmen, he was obsolescent, like old Victorio, in this suddenly civilized New Mexico. The denouement was inevitable. One night, July 15, 1881, the Kid walked into an unlighted room which he thought contained friends and was shot through the heart by Pat Garrett, who collected the $500 reward. Greater rewards went to Garrett and subsequent authors for book, stage, and film "biographies" of the Kid. (McKee, pp. 161-162).

Although President Garfield offered to reappoint Wallace Governor, he was tired of the continual upheaval, and his wife made no secret of her unhappiness there. On June 4, 1881, he turned over the Governor's Palace to Col. Lionel Sheldon, and headed home to Crawfordsville.

If *The Fair God* had a thirty-year-fuse, *Ben-Hur* had an even longer one: dating clear back to the Magian verses read by Professor Hoshour in 1840—and before that, at his mother's knee. With the completion of *The Fair God* in '72, Wallace cast about for another writing project. He chose a Christian subject for pragmatic reasons only. While he had often attended Methodist churches as a child, and later, a "Christian" chapel, he had no real convictions on the subject: "I was not in the least influenced by religious sentiment. I had no conviction about God or Christ." (McKee, p. 164).

Actually, the fuse is even better described in a little book few today have ever seen, Wallace's *The First Christmas*, Harpers 1880, 1902.

> I heard the story of the Wise Men when a small boy. My mother read it to me; and of all the tales of the Bible and the New Testament none took such a lasting hold upon my imagination, none so filled me with wonder. Who were they? Whence did they come? Were they all from the same country? Did they come singly or together? Above all, what led them to Jerusalem, asking of all they met the strange question, "Where is he that is born King of the Jews? for we have seen his star in the east, and are come to worship him."
>
> Finally I concluded to write of them. By carrying the story on to the birth of Christ in the cave by Bethlehem, it was possible, I thought, to compose a *brochure* that might be acceptable to the Harper Brothers. Seeing the opportunities it afforded for rich illustration, they might be pleased to publish it as a serial in their Magazine. When the writing was done, I laid it away in a drawer of my desk, waiting for courage to send it forward; and there it might be still lying had it not been for a fortuitous circumstance.
>
> There was a great mass Convention of Republicans at Indianapolis in '76. I resolved to attend it, and took a sleeper from Crawfordsville the evening before the meeting. Moving slowly down the aisle of the car, talking with some friends, I passed the state-room. There was a knock on the door from the inside, and some one called my name. Upon answer, the door opened, and I saw Colonel Robert G. Ingersoll looking comfortable as might be considering the sultry weather.
>
> "Was it you called me, Colonel?"
> "Yes," he said. "Come in. I feel like talking."

I leaned against the cheek of the door, and said: "Well, if you will let me dictate the subject, I will come in."
"Certainly. That's exactly what I want."
I took seat by him, and began:
"Is there a God?"
Quick as a flash, he replied: "I don't know; do you?"
And then I: "Is there a Devil?"
And he: "I don't know; do you?"
"Is there a Heaven?"
"I don't know; do you?"
"Is there a Hell?"
"I don't know; do you?"
"Is there a Hereafter?"
"I don't know; do you?"
I finished, saying, "There, Colonel, you have the texts. Now go."

And he did. He was in prime mood; and, beginning, his ideas turned to speech, flowing like a heated river. His manner of putting things was marvelous; and as the Wedding Guest was held by the glittering eye of the Ancient Mariner, I sat spellbound, listening to a medley of argument, eloquence, wit, satire, audacity, irreverence, poetry, brilliant antitheses, and pungent excoriation of believers in God, Christ, and Heaven, the like of which I had never heard. He surpassed himself, and that is saying a great deal.

The speech was brought to an end by our arrival at the Indianapolis Central Station nearly two hours after its commencement. Upon alighting from the car, we separated: he to go to a hotel, and I to my brother's, a long way up northeast of town. The street cars were at my service, but I preferred to walk, for I was in a confusion of mind not unlike dazement.

To explain this, it is necessary now to confess that my attitude with respect to religion had been one of absolute indifference. I had heard it argued times innumerable, always without interest. So, too, I had read the sermons of great preachers—Bossuet, Chalmers, Robert Hall, and Henry Ward Beecher—but always for the surpassing charm of their rhetoric. But—how strange! To lift me out of my indifference, one would think only strong affirmations of things regarded holiest would do. Yet here was I now moved as never before, and by what? The most outright denials of all human knowledge of God, Christ, Heaven, and the Hereafter which figures so in the hope and faith of the believing everywhere. Was the Colonel right? What had I on which to answer yes or no? He had made me ashamed of my ignorance; and then—here is the unexpected of the affair—as I walked on in the cool darkness I was aroused for the first time in my life to the importance of religion. To write all my reflections would require many pages. I pass them to say simply that I resolved to study the subject. And while casting round how to set about the study to the best advantage, I thought of the manuscript in my desk. Its closing scene was the child Christ in the cave by Bethlehem: why not go on with the story down to the crucifixion? That would make a book, and compel me to study everything of pertinency; after which, possibly, I would be possessed of opinions of real value.

It only remains to say that I did as resolved, with results—first, the book *Ben-Hur*, and, second, a conviction amounting to absolute belief in God and the divinity of Christ.
LEWIS WALLACE.
(*The First Christmas*, pp. iii - vii).

The Bible does not give names to the Wise Men—nor even tell us how many there were. The names we have—Caspar, Melchior, and Balthasar—come from a medieval tale (erroneously credited to the Venerable Bede). Wallace took it from there.

Early on, Wallace had immersed himself in the Library of Congress, trying to learn everything there was to know there about the Jews—then moved on to relevant history, geography, and botany. Out of all this he had come up with his "brochure" (*The First Christmas*), not published separately until 1902.

But now he was going far beyond this 20,000 word book: he wanted to create another work of the statue of *The Fair God*; with similarities to *Ivanhoe*. To do so, he needed another Prescott; he found it in Gibbon and Josephus: "combats, heroisms, oppositions of fate and fortune, characters for sympathy, characters for detestation, civilization and religion in moral issue." (McKee, p. 165).

And he bought, prodigiously, books and maps—including a huge German-printed relief map of Palestine—and hauled it all back to Indiana with him, organized it all, put up the great relief map, and started writing.

During that first year, he wrote six chapters (16,000 words), written wherever and whenever there were non-committed islands of time—he used *every available moment*. He had a bit of trouble with his characters' names, for he didn't want to commit the same sin he had in the earlier book: too many unpronounceable names. "Hur" he took from Joshua, "Messala" from Shakespeare, and "Esther" both from Scripture and from his beloved mother. He had a terrible time with the Roman galleys, ransacking libraries in both Washington and Boston until he felt confident he could perfectly conceptualize them.

Then came that incredible epiphany generated by the meeting with that famed doubter, the "Ivan" of Nineteenth Century America, Robert Ingersoll. That challenge demanded an answer; the answer would be *Ben-Hur*. The Magian brochure (*The First Christmas*), would set the stage in the first part, the Nazarene a character in the plot, and Ben-Hur would become Christ's champion, His Knight.

The hardest part was the first; what should he do with it? He decided to make it a prologue—in which both Balthasar and Christ are crystallized, and a tone set, much as would be true in a musical symphony.

Secondly, he borrowed from such masters as Balzac, Dickens, and others, who before they began their action, explained the overlapping worlds their characters lived and interacted in; in this case, describing through description and dialogue the moral, social and political conditions of that time period. Once *that* was done, the action could thunder along without explanations of any kind.

So he wrote—in courtroom, train station, and home. On summer afternoons, his favorite writing place was outside under one of his tallest beech trees. His method? He claimed to have none: he just let the scenes come to mind and then flow spontaneously.

Those who read copy early on, such as his friend Maurice Thompson, warned that the burden and challenges of governing the vast New Mexico Territory would bring the book to an untimely halt. It was then almost three-fourths done. But the Governor stayed the course: there in the dungeon-like bedroom behind the executive office in the three and a half centuries old Governor's Palace—on a rough pine table lighted by an oil lamp--, he wrote into the far reaches of the night. Mrs. Wallace worried continually that either the vengeful Billy the Kid or one of the many others who had threatened to kill him would see him silhouetted against the lamp and make the threat good. Wallace observed, "The ghosts, if they were ever about, did not disturb me; yet in the hush of that gloomy harborage I beheld the Crucifixion, and strove to write what I felt." (McKee, p. 168). The New Mexico landscape reminded him of Palestine's—dry and arid.

He experienced with Ben-Hur that return to troubled Jerusalem, the duel with the Centurion, the proclamation of Messiahship for Christ, the encounter with family,—and Calvary.

He was finished. *Judah, a Tale of the Christ* was what he decided to call it. The third and final version, he wrote in purple ink—indeed, he wrote in purple from that time on. So it came to pass, in March of 1880, seven long years after he started it, that it was *done*.

THE RACE IS ON

He took leave of absence in April, and traveled to New York. Osgood and Boston were no longer what they had been—Harpers, in New York, was the new king of publishing --, and Wallace took his precious manuscript to Joseph Henry Harper himself.

Harper's first concern had to do with whether or not he had actually made Christ a character in the story. Wallace explained how it came to be, from Ingersoll's challenge on.

Within a week, he heard that George Ripley, later to become one of Harper's greatest editors, had written as part of his editorial critique: "He is an original and powerful writer, without precedent or prototype." The Chief himself declared, "This is the most beautiful manuscript that has ever come into this house—a bold experiment to make Christ a hero that has been often tried and always failed." (McKee, p. 169).

Because "Judah" sounded a bit too close to "Judas," the title was changed to *Ben-Hur*; and the book was published November 12, 1880. Price: a dollar and a half.

For a time, it looked like *Ben-Hur* would die quickly. In the first seven months, for instance, a paltry 2,800 copies sold. Worse yet, it was all downhill from there. So much so that by the end of 1881, its short day appeared over: it wasn't moving *anywhere*. But for some strange unexplainable reason, late in '82, it began selling again—some 300 a month. Strangely, the momentum, once reversed, only gathered speed and power: 750 copies a month in '83, 1,200 copies a month in '84/'85, 4,500 copies a month in '86/'87, and by then, it was Harpers' #1 seller. It has gone on to become one of the best-sellers of all time.

In November of '84, Wallace couldn't resist passing on to his wife Grant's response: "General Grant told me today that he read it through word for word; that he began in the morning, not having read a novel in ten years, and finished it next day at noon, after reading all night." (McKee, pp. 173-4). Perhaps most significant of all, it was the first novel—with the single exception of *Uncle Tom's Cabin*—to gain the championship of ministers everywhere, thereby making a huge hole in the anti-fiction dike.

BEN-HUR AND IRIS.—*Act IV. Scene 2.*

FOUR

The Prince

I was waiting So great were the similarities between fact and fiction that many called Wallace "Ben Hur"—for there was so much of himself poured into that portrayal. But now, the book done, and launched upon the waters of the world, it no longer belonged to the author—it belonged to the *world*. Now, what should he do? He was now in his fifties—surely he had one more book in him.

Garfield started it. The President, swamped by his hectic schedule, had taken a long time to get into this book written by his old friend. When he finished, on April 19, 1881, he wrote a deeply appreciative letter, and mailed it to Santa Fe. The letter concluded with the words: "With this beautiful and reverent book you have lightened the burden of my daily life—and renewed our acquaintance which began at Shiloh." Wallace, who at that time, was almost convinced that *Ben-Hur* was a failure, was overwhelmed by the heart-felt words: "My hope in the future of the book renews itself," he wrote back.

And Garfield appreciated authors; and Wallace had cared enough to leave the Territory, come home, and campaign for him. Garfield was grateful, and offered him another term in New Mexico—when that was turned down, he then offered the consulates of Brazil, Holland, Bolivia, and Paraguay in succession, all of which Wallace turned down. Then Garfield read *Ben-Hur*, and was so inspired by a new idea that he wrote in his Journal, "I am inclined to send its author to Constantinople, where he may draw inspiration from the modern East for future literary work. . . . Wallace surprises me with his delicacy as well as his breadth of culture. I think Constantinople would give him opportunities for still greater success and I will try to give him that mission." (McKee, p. 190).

Turkey of today is a far cry from the Ottoman Empire of 1881. The Sultan/Emperor was still one of the world's greatest monarchs, as besides Turkey itself, he controlled the entire Arabian peninsula to its south, including Iraq, Syria, Jordan, and Palestine; Egypt, Libya, and Tunisia in North Africa; and Cypress, Crete, Albania, Bulgaria, and Greece to its west. Wallace knew that, and gladly accepted. To an interviewer, he gushed, "I felt the charm that Constantinople must have for every romantic mind. It was the Constantinople of Gibbon, Scott, Byron, Dumas—of baths, Muzzeins, veiled ladies in distress—a city of twenty-five centuries besides which Santa Fe was an upstart—the city of Saint Sophia, Sultan, Seraglio! In its gorgeous antique pageantry he would have a place of honor, and he had searched these forty years for just such theatric splendor."

"Across the commission as Minister Resident to Turkey, Garfield slyly wrote 'Ben-Hur' . . . . At the White House, Garfield, in his cordial boyish way, put his arm over Wallace's shoulder and said, 'I expect another book out of you. Your official duties will not be too onerous to allow you to write it. Locate it in Constantinople.'" (McKee, p.191).

Three months later, Garfield was dead of an assassin's bullet. But . . . , had it not been for him, there would be no *Prince of India*.

The Wallaces had always yearned to experience Europe and the East—now they were heading to an empire that straddled *three* continents! They were to be the last to see it in its glory for already European powers were beginning to dismember it, piece by piece. By Wallace's death, a bare 24 years later, Turkey would be but a shadow of what he had known. Both Wallaces looked out at European coastline passing by, and felt a euphoria hard to describe in mere words. Mrs. Wallace was not only a poetess and writer herself, but "helpmeet, amanuensis, the one who cherished clippings, documents, correspondence, souvenirs, etc., and she held her own too. For instance, her husband had dedicated *Ben-Hur* to her ("to the wife of my youth"), but so many women wrote Wallace, wishing to be "The Wife of His Maturity," that she put her foot down—subsequent editions sported a second line: "Who still abides with me."

Enroute, they toured London and Paris, and, finally, there ahead in the mist's were the domes and minarets of that great and ancient city! But they waited for several months before Wallace could be presented to the Emperor.

>A reception by the Sultan was fixed for September 6, 1881. Wallace invited Cox and Grosvenor to attend as members of the ministerial suite. A caique skimmed in greatest pomp, the Stars and Stripes billowing about Mehemet's bedizened form, ten caiquedjis rowing valorously in crimson fezzes, voluminous white shelvars, and tiny scarlet jackets, gold-embroidered. Wallace was the center of the tableau in his major general's two-starred full-dress uniform, erect and soldierly, his dress sword flashing in the afternoon sun. The crush hats ands swallow tails of Heap, Cox, Bigelow, and Grosvenor supplied a somber background.

>The landing place was the marble quay of gleaming Dolma Baghtcheh Palace, an Oriental wedding cake beside the waters. At the portal stood the indispensable Gargiulo, consuls and vice-consuls who were to swell the suite, and a crowd of petty officials. Ibrahim Bey, one of the imperial chamberlains, in a gilt-encrusted uniform, conducted them up the crystal stairway and through halls rich with

inlaid work to a spacious room of alabaster. While they awaited the court carriages, coffee and cigarettes were served. Wallace surveyed broad tables of malachite, lapis, lazuli, vert antigque; heavy, ruglike curtains, incredibly large mirrors, candelabra of coruscating cut glass. It was a proper setting for the Thespian, the author of *The Fair God, Commodus*, and *Ben-Hur*, and he accepted it with easy grace.

But they were kept waiting, five minutes, ten minutes. Wallace had been informed of the Sultan's shrewd custom of compelling new envoys to cool their heels. The intrepid Indianian, however, had his own sense of drama. He turned to Gargiulo:

"Please say to his excellency, Ibrahim Bey, that I wish to know why the carriages are not here."

The courier was astonished and confused; such a question violated the program.

"They are coming," replied the chamberlain to the formidable-looking American. "They are coming."

A moment later: "Please say to his excellency that I do not wish to wait."

"But they are here! They are here!" exclaimed the flustered chamberlain.

Anxiously he led the way to the courtyard. The carriages had been there a long time, but would have been there longer had not Wallace challenged protocol. The incident went down in diplomatic history.

The procession to Yildiz, a mile away, was impressive. Thirty mounted zaptiehs, their guns pointed to the front, right, and left, galloped in advance. An especially large steed bravely bore Mehemet. Behind clattered four gold-and-satin carriages, Wallace and Gargiulo occupying the first, most elaborate one. A score of zaptiehs brought up the rear.

From the kiosk's portals a detachment of the Sultan's private guard escorted the party to the main doorway. They were welcomed to the reception room by the empire's dignitaries: Osman Pasha, minister of war, heavy-set, gallant defender of Plevna; Assim Pasha, minister of foreign affairs; Osman Bey, first chamberlain; Munir Pasha, master of ceremonies. Nubian slaves brought more cigarettes and coffee; the saucers were of solid gold encrusted with diamonds. When His Majesty was ready, they marched into the capacious throne room. At the far end stood a frail man of medium height, in European costume except for the inevitable crimson fez. He had a hooked nose, thin lips, full beard; his face wore a dark pallor, and he looked dejected. He was Sultan Abdul-Hamid Khan II, aged thirty-eight, absolute monarch of fifty million subjects, Caliph of two hundred million, "Great Assassin" of Armenians. He was twenty-first in direct descent from Osman Khan I, who had founded this reigning house in the year 1300; he counted among his personal possessions two hundred and fifty wives, fifteen hundred women servants, two hundred carriages, six hundred horses, one hundred and fifty coachmen, twenty palaces. Numbers of his family had succumbed to the bowstring and other curious devices. He was an Arabian Nights caliph living in an Arabian Nights environment.

Wallace and Gargiulo advanced within a few yards of the Sultan and, with the suite, made a deep bow. In a whisper Assim Pasha prompted his imperial master. Abdul-Hamid expressed in almost inaudible tones his pleasure at the meeting and his interest in the United States; Assim Pasha repeated this in Turkish to Gargiulo, who conveyed an

English version to Wallace. The new minister thereupon presented his credentials, with proper reference to amicable relations and to his predecessor; his words reached the Sultan through the two intermediaries, sentence by sentence. Wallace then asked and received permission to present each member of his suite.

Every word so far had followed a set formula. There ensued some less formal conversation, in the course of which the Sultan asked about President Garfield. Wallace said the news was better but not encouraging. The interview was now to close; but Wallace saw opportunity for drama, and seized it.
"And now," said he to Gargiulo, "say to his imperial majesty that as representative of the American people I desire to take his majesty's hand."

Consternation. Turks did not shake hands even with one another. For an infidel, a giaour, to aspire to touch the Padishah's hand was sacrilegious presumption.

"But!" exclaimed Gargiulo, looking less swarthy.

"Say it," commanded Wallace.

Gargiulo spoke to Assim Pasha, who was thunderstruck.

"What is it?" broke in the Sultan. "What does his excellency say?"

Prostrate at the monarch's feet, Assim Pasha with much circumlocution relayed the unheard-of request. Abdul-Hamid was momentarily puzzled. Then, faintly smiling, he stepped forward and shook Wallace's hand. It was the first time in the six-hundred-year history of sultans that one of them had clasped the palm of a giaour.

Protocol regained its sway, and coffee circulated again in the reception room. "But," recorded Professor Grosvenor as another incident went down in diplomatic history, "in the social atmosphere a new element had entered, invisible, but felt. It made itself recognized in the furtive and bewildered glances which those exalted minions of an Oriental system cast upon the strange man from the West, who had overridden tradition, and as an equal had pressed their sovereign's hand. The minister was to hold many more interviews with the sultan. But in that first interview he had impressed his verile personality upon Abdul-Hamid. (McKee, pp. 197-200).

That was but the beginning: from that time on, Wallace was a man set apart in the imperial city. He and the Sultan gradually developed a deep respect and friendship for each other. They smoked, dined, and drank coffee together. A summons from His Majesty might come any time—in the middle of day or in the dead of night --, seeking counsel or just a companion. The Sultan continually tried to press lavish gifts upon him, but American protocol forbade it. Abdul-Hamid couldn't help but notice how enthralled Wallace was with the exotic pageantry of court and capital city. And he appreciated too the personal inscription in the copy of *Ben-Hur* he gave him. The Wallaces explored *everywhere*, and were even privileged to be invited into the Seraglio, the Tile Palace, the Sacred Residence, the Hall of the Divan, the Nine Kitchens, the Inner Seraglio, the Chamber of Supplication, the Throne Room, the Treasure House (with the world's largest emerald), the Library, and so on.

Later that year, they took a two-month trip into the Holy Land (by steamer to Jaffa and by caravan to Jerusalem).

> At Bethany, Wallace dismounted and followed Ben-Hur's exact route up Mount Olivet. He fancied he found the very

stone on which his hero had sat. "I went down into the old Valley of Kedron," he later recalled with pride, "and from the old well of Enrogel looked over the valley, and every feature of the scene appeared identical with the description of that which the hero of the story looked upon. At every point of the journey over which I traced his steps to Jerusalem, I found the descriptive details true to the existing objects and scenes, and I find no reason for making a single change in the text of the book." The solitary error he ever acknowledged in *Ben-Hur* did not relate to the Holy Land, but to the eruption of Vesuvius, which actually occurred four years later than he said in the story.

The party lunched near the Pool of Solomon and lodged in tents at Hebron, avoiding an insect-infested khan. Next day they inspected Hebron and various mosques to which they had entree by virtue of the sultan's firman; only four Christians—the Prince of Wales, his two sons, and Francis Joseph of Austria—had been before them in one of the mosques. At Bethlehem they surveyed the bare, burned hill up which Joseph and Mary once toiled, and its road, white with chalky dust. They followed the leader through streets swarming with beggars, and galleries where tapers had to be lighted, to the manger. They dined with the Greek Patriarch in the Church of the Nativity, camped near Mar Saba, where banished monks would not permit women to enter their monastery, tasted the Dead Sea's bitter water, cooled their foreheads in the Jordan, tented at Jericho, and reëntered Jerusalem. (McKee, p. 205).

Then they traveled by rail to Cairo—Egypt was now in English hands --, traveled down the Nile to Memphis . . . and on back to Constantinople.

1883 was a high year for Wallace—for the first time in 35 years, he was out of debt. Thanks to his book sales, he was now able to save much of the government salary he was receiving

($7,500 a year, plus $3,000), a very large sum of money in those days. In the fall, they spent two months in Italy.

By 1884, he was beginning to long for home . . . but it was not until spring of '85 that he was cleared to return to America. But Abdul-Hamid didn't want him to leave, and offered him whatever it would take to keep him there, in his own employ . . . but, by then, Wallace himself had changed. He no longer had anything to prove to anyone. He, too, had become the Prince he had always idealized. Thanks to his book income, he was at last free.

The Sultan asked him to stay in touch by letter, at least once a month, and Wallace promised—leaving behind him a huge English mastiff pup which he had secured in England. The Sultan adored it. On his part, the Sultan bestowed him four parting gifts—which he could now accept: an album of palace photographs; a painting of a Turkish princess Wallace had admired; a solid gold cigarette box, the lid set with twenty solitaire diamonds and initialed 'S.H.'; and the awarding of the ancient decoration, First Class of the Order Imperiale Medjidie (an award going back half a millennium).

At the last, the Sultan, assailed on every side much as wolves close in on a wounded animal, made a touching farewell speech:

> I regard you as more than a Minister. Since I have been on the throne, no foreigner has come to me officially or in private capacity for whom I have had the friendship I have for you. If you will look back on our relationship, you must see that I am speaking in earnest. I find it difficult to part with you. I would like you to remain with me, and have already offered you honorable service. I regret you declined the offer, but it is natural that you should prefer life in your own country. (McKee. p. 216).

The new book, he had started almost as soon as he had arrived in Turkey. His four years there were full of note-taking and expeditions here and there; gathering insights and information.

Returned from the great imperial city on the Sea of Marmara, Wallace found that somehow, some way, the lustre of his appointment, tied in with his own literary attainments, had raised him to an unprecedented eminence. And the excesses, abuses, and scandals of the Grant administration, had resulted in a more level playing field Civil War-wise. From now until the end of his life, he "attended and spoke at a staggering total of reunions. . . . Legion assembles, Eleventh Indiana Division roll calls, Memorial Day exercises, encampments at Shiloh, Cincinnati, Monocacy, Washington. First and last, they thrilled him with the old music, the old words, the old faces, the old uniforms. It was a pageantry of which he never tired, which in fact grew brighter as the restless yearnings of the past were quenched in the new role." (McKee, p. 234).

He made the cover of *Harper Magazine*, he was appointed to the inspecting boards of both West Point and the Annapolis Naval Academy. He was offered the Brazilian consulate again, and turned it down again. He was home now, and meant to remain there. One last quest he had: to complete the mission Garfield sent him on: write a book set in Constantinople.

As his central character, he chose the beautiful and pious Princess Irene (borrowed from Knolles' work), "beloved of both Constantine and Prince Mahomed." (McKee, p. 237). The wandering Jew would be another central character. Gradually he built a large historical library from which he created the setting, plot, and action. He finished the book twelve years after the Presidential mandate, on January 23 of '93. He had originally planned to dedicate the book to the Sultan . . . but decided, at the last minute, to dedicate it to his father, David Wallace, instead, dead now for many years—but always, in memory, his shining ideal. The final title was *The Prince of India; or Why Constantinople Fell*; and it was a 300,000 word blockbuster of a novel. The hero, the Prince, walks the global stage—much as did Wallace himself. And these days, Wallace was labeled "The Prince" by those who knew him. When he walked into a room or an auditorium, still ramrod straight, in his Major General uniform, flashing sword, and on his chest the imperial decoration—it was indeed, as a prince.

The book sold well: 100,000 copies during the first six months—then slowed --, but eventually reached 200,000 sales.

With his last opus maximus done, with his long and illustrious military and political career ebbing to a close, it was time to revel in life and the adulation that now poured in on him in wave after wave. Everywhere he went, he was wrapped in the growing excitement over *Ben-Hur*. In Crawfordsville, he now had constructed his long dreamed of palatial study—there he wrote, puttered, and dreamed the hours away.

And he was there in New York to experience that incredible first night when "Ben Hur" was brought to life on an epic stage for the first time. There, the center of all eyes, the old warrior, with heart undimmed by the years.

On the morning of February 15, 1905, he told Mrs. Lane, "I am going . . . but I am not afraid." That evening, he counseled his grandchildren and gave them his patriarchal blessing, then bade a last farewell to his sister-in-law, son, and "The Wife of his Youth."

And then—knowing his Lord—the Prince died.

Joseph Leininger Wheeler, Ph.D.
The Grey House
Conifer, Colorado

AFTERWORD

Discussions With Professor Wheeler

(For Formal School, Home School, and Book Club Discussions)

Note: NOT TO BE STUDIED UNTIL BOOK AND BIOGRAPHY HAVE BEEN READ

It is perhaps safe to say that one's life can never be the same again after reading a book like *Ben-Hur*. Certainly mine has not been. Discussion-wise, the book is almost inexhaustible for in it Wallace tackles all life, both on this earth and in the hereafter.

Discussion Questions

1. What is the impact of the book spiritually (on one's walk with God)?

2. What are the insights you gained about history, the ancient world? What were your biggest surprises?

3. How would you compare life back then to life today? What different? What the same?

4. Who are the strongest characters in the book? Why? How are they developed?

5. How reverently do you feel Christ is presented in the story? Does the book help to make Him more real?

6. Scripture helps us very little in terms of telling us what Christ looked like physically, consequently all descriptions are purely conjecture. Some authorities -- such as Bruce Barton in his book *The Man Nobody Knows* -- portrays Christ as robust, macho. Others -- such as Wallace in this book -- portray Christ as being a little effeminate. So what do you think He was like? Reasons?

7. What crossovers did you notice in terms of Lew Wallace in the bio and the book itself? What aspects of his actual life do you feel he mined the most extensively in writing the book?

8. What is the role of Balthasar in the book? How would it be different without Him?

9. In great literature, there is almost always significant character growth and change. Take the key characters and plot them out. Which ones change the most? Why? Which ones least? Why? Overall impact?

10. Discuss in depth the two expectations of Christ in His earthly ministry: Messiah father-figure versus Political Leader - King. Sort them out.

11. An unabridged dictionary is almost an essential in completely understanding this book. If the reader is to grow vocabulary-wise something else is needed *besides* the dictionary -- vocabulary

cards. On one side, the word; on the other is a definition and the word used in a sentence. Every time you stumble on words you are unsure of -- and I found quite a number myself! --, then it's time to make out a card for it. Continually go over these cards; and keep all except those you never miss on in a card file. You will be amazed at how fast your vocabulary will grow!

12. Find out all you can about Rabbi Hillel, perhaps -- other than Christ -- the greatest Jewish thought-leader of all time. Perhaps you have heard of Hillel's Eight Magic Words:
    "If not now - when?"
    "If not me -- whom?"
Those two questions have been with us for two milleniums; and, speaking just for myself, my life has never been the same since I internalized them (saying them over and over to myself, day after day, week after week, until they become a permanent part of my psyche). I guarantee that, if you internalize them as I have done, those two questions will revolutionalize your life.

13. What about the subject of vengeance? Contrast Ben-Hur, in this respect, to Christ. What lessons can we learn?

14. There's quite a bit in the book about life coming full circle: as we do unto others will, sooner or later be done unto us -- usually with compound interest.
    What lessons can we learn here -- especially from the life of Iras?

15. Ought there to be a pecking order in our friendships? In other words, are *any* of us more important than any of the rest of us? In Christ's eyes?

Now compare your conclusions to real life around you -- especially *you*. Do *you* treat some people with more kindness and respect than you do others? Why?

16. There was considerable discussion -- especially with Simonides -- about the impact of great wealth on people. What conclusions did he reach? Had he not turned over everything to Ben-Hur, do you think Esther would have been treated differently? Why?
On a lesser scale of wealth, is it wise to give everything to one's children? Why? What happens when that occurs?

17. There is a lot in the book about treatment of one's father, mother, and family. What lessons do we learn in that respect during the course of the book?

18. There are many different concepts around the world -- and even within Christianity -- about what a "soul" is. There's a whole chapter on it in this book. What do *you* think it is?

19. Along with it, there is also considerable discussion of fame. Why is it that each of us, from babyhood on, tends to grandstand, to show off? We do and say all kinds of things in our obsession to be noticed. And none of us wants to die without having first achieved some kind of recognition or immortality of some kind.
Discuss this issue at depth.

20. Discuss at length love and romance as portrayed in the book. Especially get into the irrationality of love. Why is it so difficult to really get to *know* one of the opposite sex? Note all the years Ben-Hur was associated with Iras. Did he know what she was really like because of it? What about the values he was looking

for? Contrast with those Esther has, and Iras? How does one know when the right one comes along?

There is a great deal in the Wallace bio which has to do with Wallace's perception of women, love, romance, and the role of a wife. Then he stirs in his own romance, courtship, marriage, and long life with his wife. Today, with one out of every two marriages ending in divorce, what lessons can we learn from Wallace's own life? And compare the real life to the fictional one depicted in *Ben-Hur*.

What are the qualities he values most? How do these compare to those our society emphasizes most.

There is very little overt sexuality in either the bio or in *Ben-Hur*. Does its absence weaken the book? Today, sexuality appears to be an end in itself, almost a form of aerobics or Olympic performance. Sex divorced from caring commitment appears to be almost a national norm. Discuss the implications and what we can do to reverse the tide.

21. Be sure and write thoughts, reactions, tangents, etc. *each day* in your journal as you read the book. Now that you are through with the book, what benefits do you see from faithfully writing in your journal?

22. Lew Wallace himself -- in bio --, how did he change during his lifetime?

23. What is it about externals? Wallace deals with this quite a bit in the book. What is the role of beauty in our lives?

24. What results from having so much money you don't have to work? How happy does it make one to have wealth? Tie in the young rich in Antioch who associated with Messala.

25. Discuss leprosy then -- and now. Do we have any counterparts today? Notice that in those days you were ostracized if you were (a) a leper, (b) poor, (c) blind, (d) childless. Compare to how we treat people today.

26. Make a habit of writing down in your journal or on cards quotations that are provocative and memorable. Same with similes and metaphors. Sometimes you will have to adapt them a little in order to make them aphoristic.

The following are examples, and will also provide you with additional discussion material.

QUOTATIONS

- "Yet -- if in their passing, men stop to wring all the nonsense out of their lives, what threadbare rags they would be left holding." (Wallace *Autobiography*)
- "Revenge the passion is a disease of the heart which climbs up, up to the brain, and feeds itself on both alike."
- "Power is a fretful thing, and hath its wings always spread for flight."
- "Man as a subject is the ambition for a king; the soul of a man for its salvation is the desire of a God."
- "Beauty is of itself is a power."
- "A man is never so on trial as in the moment of excessive good fortune."
- "When God walks the earth, his steps are often centuries apart."
- "Would you hurt a man keenest, strike at his self love; would you hurt a woman most, aim at her affections."
- "Riches take wings, comforts vanish, hope withers away, but love stays with us. Love is God."

- "It is not often we have hearts roomy enough for more than one of the absorbing passions at the same time; in its blaze the others may continue to live, but only as lesser lights."

FIGURES OF SPEECH

- "Forth from each stall, like missiles in a volly from so many great guns, rushed the six fours." (Simile)
- "Apprehension always paints in black." (Metaphor)
- "If you cook the meal with words, I will promise an ocean of butter." (Metaphor)
- ". . . if at the roots of thy tongue there is a lie in coil." (Metaphor)
- "Suspicions are weeds of the mind which grow of themselves, and most rapidly when least wanted." (Metaphor)
- " . . . so loved that the near stars rattled like seeds in a parched pod." (Simile)

27. To those who have both read the book and seen one or both of the "Ben-Hur" movies, in what ways do the movies differ from the book? Where does the plot differ? Notice the difference in the '59 film when Iras is left out. Is the movie faithful to the book in spirit -- or does it radically change the emphasis? Which is better: book or movie? Why?

ABOUT THE AUTHOR

Joe Wheeler, Ph.D., is professor emeritus of English at Washington Adventist University, general editor at Focus on the Family, and cofounder and executive director of the International Zane Grey's West Society. Besides the best-selling *Christmas in My Heart®* series, Wheeler has also edited the *Great Stories Remembered, Heart to Heart, Forged in the Fire*, and *The Good Lord Made Them All* series. He is also one of America's leading story anthologizers (this is his seventy-ninth story anthology and his ninety-fourth book). Dr. Wheeler resides in Conifer, Colorado, with his wife and publishing partner, Connie.

ABOUT THE PUBLISHER

FH Publishers is a division of FaithHappenings.com

FaithHappenings.com is the premier, first-of-its kind, online Christian resource that contains an array of valuable local and national faith-based information all in one place. Our mission is "to inform, enrich, inspire and mobilize Christians and churches while enhancing the unity of the local Christian community so they can better serve the needs of the people around them." FaithHappenings.com will be the primary i-Phone, Droid App/Site and website that people with a traditional Trinitarian theology will turn to for national and local information to impact virtually every area of life.

The vision of FaithHappenings.com is to build the vibrancy of the local church with a true "one-stop-resource" of information and events that will enrich the soul, marriage, family, and church life for people of faith. We want people to be touched by God's Kingdom, so they can touch others FOR the Kingdom.

Find out more at www.faithhappenings.com.

Other books to come in the **Classic Author Biography Series** in 2016 and 2017:

- Charles Dickens and *A Christmas Carol*
- Abbie Farwell Brown and *The Christmas Angel*
- Daniel Defoe and *Robinson Crusoe* (including *Farther Adventures*)
- Louisa May Alcott and *Little Women* (including *Little Men*)
- Lucy Maud Montgomery and *Anne of Green Gables*
- Henryk Sienkiewicz and *Quo Vadis*
- Grace Richmond and *The Twenty-Four of June*
- Gene Stratton-Porter and *Freckles*
- Charles Dickens and *David Copperfield*

www.ingramcontent.com/pod-product-compliance
Lightning Source LLC
Chambersburg PA
CBHW031648040426
42453CB00006B/244